A PEDAGOGY OF KIND

MW01035294

TEACHING, ENGAGING, AND THRIVING IN HIGHER ED

James M. Lang and Michelle D. Miller, SERIES EDITORS

A PEDAGOGY OF KINDNESS

CATHERINE J. DENIAL

University of Oklahoma Press : Norman

Library of Congress Cataloging-in-Publication Data

Names: Denial, Catherine J., 1971– author.
Title: A pedagogy of kindness / Catherine J. Denial.
Description: Norman : University of Oklahoma Press, [2024]. | Series:
    Teaching, engaging, and thriving in higher ed ; volume 1 | Includes
    bibliographical references and index. | Summary: "Articulating a fresh vision
    for teaching, one that focuses on ensuring justice, believing people, and
    believing in people, this how-to offers evidence-based insights and draws
    from the author's own rich experiences as a professor to provide practical
    tips for reshaping syllabi, assessing student performance, and creating trust
    and belonging in the classroom"—Provided by publisher.
Identifiers: LCCN 2023053653 | ISBN 978-0-8061-9384-7 (hardcover) |
    ISBN 978-0-0861-9385-4 (paperback)
Subjects: LCSH: College teaching—Methodology. | College students—United
    States—Social conditions. | Education, Higher—Social aspects—United
    States. | Kindness. | BISAC: EDUCATION / Philosophy, Theory & Social
    Aspects | EDUCATION / Schools / Levels / Higher
Classification: LCC LB2331 .D426 2024 | DDC 378.1/7—dc23/eng/20240309
LC record available at https://lccn.loc.gov/2023053653

A Pedagogy of Kindness is Volume 1 in the Teaching, Engaging, and Thriving in
    Higher Ed series.

The paper in this book meets the guidelines for permanence and durability of
the Committee on Production Guidelines for Book Longevity of the Council on
Library Resources, Inc. ⊗

For Mr. Winter, who taught me about World War I poetry when I was eight, and for Mr. Schofield, who taught me working-class history when I was fifteen

CONTENTS

Acknowledgments   ix

Introduction   1

1. Kindness toward the Self   15

2. Kindness and the Syllabus   40

3. Kindness and Assessment   59

4. Kindness in the Classroom   81

Conclusion   101

Notes   105

Bibliography   129

Index   147

ACKNOWLEDGMENTS

Writing a book during the COVID-19 pandemic, with all its attendant personal and professional pressures, while supporting incredible students through one of the most challenging periods of our lives, was difficult. Without the direction, cheerleading, and support of many dozens of people, it would have been impossible. It is with immense gratitude that I pause to celebrate the friends and colleagues without whom this text would be only an idea.

I was supported in writing this book by both the Mary Elizabeth Hand Bright and Edwin Winslow Bright and the Edgar S. and Ruth W. Burkhardt funds at Knox College. These funds made it possible for me to attend the Digital Pedagogy Lab in 2017, and I owe a debt of gratitude to the organizers, stream leaders, and attendees at that institute. I'm grateful to Chris Friend, Sean Michael Morris, and Jesse Stommel for all that they shared. I'm further grateful to Chris Friend, who, as the editor of *Hybrid Pedagogy*, gave *A Pedagogy of Kindness* its first home.

Josh Eyler was the first person to suggest to me that kindness and pedagogy deserved a book-length treatment. I am forever grateful for his confidence in this work, and to Derek Krissoff, Andrew Berzanskis, and all the incredible staff at the University of Oklahoma Press who shepherded this project to completion with patience, creativity, and compassion. James Lang, one of the two editors of this series, challenged me and encouraged me to realize the kind of book this could be. I'm also grateful to my anonymous reviewer, whose erudite suggestions made this a better book. I have unending gratitude for David Chesanow's meticulous copyediting, and Ben Shaw for his indexing skills. Jessamyn Neuhaus and Yvonne Seale read almost every chapter of this manuscript and offered incredible support, critique, and encouragement. Ann Gagné offered generous feedback on a key section of this book related to disability; she is one of my most valued teachers. I have learned from every group of faculty and staff with whom I've interacted over Zoom and in person over the last five years: thank you for your generative and creative questions. All remaining mistakes are, of course, my own.

I wrote much of this book in Zoom companionship with Courtney Joseph, without whom I might never have found my forward momentum. I am also tremendously grateful to Beth Godbee, Candace Epps-Robertson, and all my fellow writers in the Tuesday and Friday Heart-Head-Hands online writing groups I've attended over the last three years. I could not have written this book without the fellowship and encouragement you offered. Thank you, also, to Marisol Pineda Conde for arriving in my life with such beautiful questions at exactly the right moment.

At Knox College, I have been constantly challenged and uplifted by the friendship of Mary Armon, Deirdre Dougherty, Ben Farrer, Jennifer Foubert, Gina Franco, Hilary Lehman, and Gabrielle Raley-Karlin. I am grateful to everyone who has shown me the very best side of being in community in and around higher ed: Cathy Adams, Kelly Baker, Joshua Barnes, Sharon Block, Kai Campbell, Sarah Rose Cavanagh, David Chang, Karen Costa, sarah madoka currie, Andrew Dell'Antonio, Elizabeth Drummond, Kate Elliott, Andrew J. Farrell, Anne Gagné, Kevin Gannon, Teresa Gonzales, Deb Harkness, Jennifer Hart, Angela Keysor, Travis Chi Wing Lau, Liz Lehfeldt, Micah Logan, Jennifer Morgan, Michelle Moyd, Jason Nethercut, Jacki Rand, Viji Sathy, Sarah Scullin, Jennifer Sessions, Jane Simonsen, Clarissa Sorensen-Unruh, Rachel Stern-Lockerman, Rebecca Weaver, Bridgett Williams-Searle, and Karin Wulf. I have learned so much from the conversations among educators on Twitter, from each and every fellow of the Bright Institute at Knox College since 2018, and from my fellow collaborators in the Mellon-funded "Pedagogies, Communities, and Practices of Care in the Academy after Covid-19" project.

My Knox students are at the very heart of this book; you have been some of my most important teachers. Particular gratitude goes to Josh Althoff, Selina Aviles, Allie Bird, Johanna Blume, Maggie Cheng, Liliana Coelho, James Cook, Sophie Croll, Celinda Davis, Teagan Eastman, Kylie Hoang, Mary Houlihan, Kate Hovda, Jordan Hurst, Olivia Keneipp, Rebecca Lauer, Forrest Marie Linsell, Eva Marley, Anna Meier, Ai Miller, Amanda Mitchell, Maricruz Osario, Sarah Pawlicki, Courtney Pletcher, Laura Pochodylo, Gabrielle Rajerison, GraceAnne Roach, Janyl Romero, Kristal Romero, Mia Rousonelos, Eden Sarkisian, Tim Schmeling, Jarrod Showalter, Margaret Spiegel, and Janie Sutherd.

My friends have sustained me through all the ups and downs of the last several years. Megan Scott is my irreplaceable partner in appreciating all the finer things in life (comedy, corgis, wine, Luca Marinelli), and

Ann Marie McNamara is the very definition of "family." Laura Sayles knows me inside and out; Christian Crouch is an unending source of wisdom and joy; Tamika Nunley is warmth and sunlight. My Friday happy hour Zoom buddies are a sustaining gift: Rachel Barenblat, Shannon Farley, Sandy Ryan, and Tisha Turk. Linda Ruscionelli and Lex Scott have helped me keep body and soul together; Nikki Malley understands me to my core; Melinda Jones-Rhoades teaches me how to keep doing the things that matter. I cannot say enough wonderful things about Jenn Dowell, Laura Jones, Jake Marcet, Caitlin Muelder, Jess Shipley, and Brian Tibbets. To those I have forgotten, I beg your forgiveness and promise to buy you the beverage of your choice when next we meet.

To my beloved niblings, Clara and Willa, I hope that you continue to love learning throughout your lives and that your teachers lead with kindness. To my family in England and Germany, I send love.

INTRODUCTION

In the past few years, whenever I've been asked to sum up my approach to pedagogy, I've said, "Kindness."

Academia is not, by and large, a kind place. The engine of higher ed is fueled by stories of individualism, competition, prestige, and distrust. The solitary genius, working away in their office or their lab, is lauded for single-minded devotion to their craft, a discreet veil drawn over their personal privilege and over the family members, service workers, and administrative staff who make that "solitary" career possible. Systemic problems aren't often recognized as such, much less met with systemic solutions. Rooting out the ableism that has been baked into academia since its inception and changing the cultural norms about knowledge production and communication that define higher ed are tasks passed over in favor of issuing individual accommodation forms to students. The specific racial prejudices that have historically undergirded the development of higher ed in the United States—through the on-campus labor of enslaved men, women, and children; by profits derived from slavery and colonization; by the drive to assimilate Native students and "civilize" them—are rarely woven into present-day curricula. And teaching is too often neglected as an enterprise that requires training as well as financial and career support. Culturally, we insert a generalized suspicion of students—they'll cheat; they won't do the reading; they'll never come to class!—into the space where pedagogical training should reside.

There are people in the world who consider kindness insufficient to meet these challenges and the responsibilities we shoulder in the classroom, much less the wider world. Many think this way because people confuse kindness with the idea of "being nice"—of being agreeable in all circumstances, of masking disagreement, of refusing to ripple the waters in our institutions and professions. But real kindness is not about individual pleasantries or letting injustices pass. Niceness, in contrast to compassion, is often *unkind*, a Band-Aid we're urged to plaster over deep fissures in our institutions, wielded as a weapon instead of as a balm. Niceness doesn't ask a lot of questions about precarity in our profession, the financial burden of education, the treatment of historically excluded students, or the uncompensated, additional practical and emotional labor asked of women and genderqueer individuals of all races and men of color in education. Politicians, "thought leaders," and industry professionals bring pressures to bear on our classrooms from outside them, generating a nationwide clamor for standardization, testing, and rote assessment. Because of this we're more likely to hear from leaders in our fields about standards and rigor than kindness. (My national professional organization says, for example, that "good teaching entails accuracy and rigor" but never mentions compassion.)[1]

In contrast to niceness, kindness is real, it's honest, and it demands integrity. It's unkind to mislead people or lie to them, for example, meaning that kindness necessitates tough conversations. Boundaries, too, are a form of kindness, a way of respecting and honoring our physical and mental energy so that we do not deplete ourselves in the service of others. Shifting our practice toward kindness is not always painless; as bell hooks memorably wrote in *Teaching to Transgress*, "There can be, and usually is, some degree of pain involved in giving up old ways of thinking and knowing and learning new approaches."[2] But here's what a pedagogy of kindness is not: It's not about sacrificing ourselves and our well-being. It's not about taking on more emotional labor (at least, not unless you're someone who is rarely called on to do any emotional labor at all). It's not about complicating teaching even further. It's about reorienting ourselves to a new way of thinking so that it strips away much of the burdensome work we've been imposing on ourselves for so long. And here's what a pedagogy of kindness most definitely is: It's about attending to justice, believing people, and believing *in* people. It's a discipline.

I didn't always think this way. Like almost everyone, I was socialized into an academia that focused on individual achievement, competition, and distrust rather than kindness. When I first stepped into a higher-ed classroom, I was a working-class, first-generation, international graduate student who had earned a BA in American studies exactly one month before. I didn't know the word "pedagogy," much less have any idea that there were choices I could make about how to approach teaching. I knew almost nothing about the American education system, as I was in the United States on an exchange fellowship awarded by my undergraduate institution. (I had applied to the program to see the world a little, not because I knew what was involved in working toward a master's degree.) Although I spent five days being trained to teach, I retain no specific memory of what I was taught—only the general impression that I should not trust my students, as they would try to get away with almost anything. My lasting impression was one of feeling entirely overwhelmed. After bleakly considering my fate, I decided that the only way I could work up the courage to do my job was to pretend to be Dana Scully from *The X-Files*, a woman who would take charge, brook no nonsense, and bring a healthy skepticism to the proceedings. (I am living proof of the old adage to fake it till you make it.)

At my next institution, educator training came in the form of workshops run by senior graduate students for their junior colleagues. I was encouraged to think of students as antagonists, always trying to get one over on their instructors. I was urged to be on the lookout for plagiarism, to be vigilant for cheaters, to assume that the students wouldn't do the reading, and to expect to be treated as a cog in the consumerist machine by students who would challenge their grades on a whim. I was once advised by a senior graduate student to "be a bitch" on the first day of class so that my students never wanted that version of myself to show up again. I was a stickler for deadlines and memorably once refused to excuse the absence of a student who was battling a burst pipe in his house when class was in session. I look back on my lack of compassion now and wince.

My early years as a graduate instructor were defined by fear. My cohort and I lacked institutional power and yet were on the front lines of teaching undergraduate students. While the leaders of the pedagogy workshops in which we participated were often white men, many of the rest of us were women and genderqueer individuals from a range of racial backgrounds and men of color. The particular challenges we faced in establishing our credentials in the classroom went undiscussed; no one offered any model for facilitating student learning that didn't depend on establishing total, unbending authority. I was afraid of screwing up, afraid of student evaluations that could, at least theoretically, make or break my funding for the next year, and afraid of not being what my students needed.[3]

Yet I was also dazzled by teaching. There was nothing quite like the moments when it all worked, when things clicked into place and my students and I had conversations that expanded the boundaries of what we knew. I learned I had a knack for spotting confusion among my students and figuring out the steps that would help smooth it out. I worked at discussion questions until they gained enough speed to lift us off the ground, generating conversations about topics I loved. I learned by trial and error; I made mistakes and survived them. I got better and better at what I did and, in time, enjoyed myself.

But things got complicated when I became a professor. I had PTSD, formally diagnosed in 2006, but in reality a companion for many years before that. I received lackluster treatment from my primary care physician and so I found myself trying to steer a course through the pressures of a new position while also battling flashbacks, dissociation, and physical pain. It never occurred to me to be kind to myself, and academia never modeled such an approach; it therefore did not occur to me to be kind to others. I put my head down and muscled my way through, and that showed up in every decision I made about teaching. I had a draconian attendance policy, and there were very few ways in which a student could earn an excused absence. In one of the two courses I was allotted during my first term at Knox (an institution that has a trimester system), I lectured for every moment of every class. When I asked if students had questions, I got resounding silence punctuated by a few queries that seemed, to me, to be strangely hostile. I thought of myself as someone training people to be historians and interpreted that in the most literal way possible; my students had to write book reviews, for example, in the style of major journals in my field. I white-knuckled it through each class session and resented every piece of grading I had to complete.

All of this came to a head during an exchange I had with a student in my lecture-only class. This student communicated, through sighs and body language, just how much he was not enjoying his experience in my course, and so I asked him to visit me during office hours so that we could talk about how we could work to change things. I posed the question, and he looked at me witheringly before saying, "You're just not Knox material."

I was stunned at the time and took his reply as evidence of his entitlement; surely he was exactly who I had been warned about in graduate school. Yet his stereotypes about academic expertise and who should be a professor notwithstanding, he was inadvertently telling something important, although it took me some time to accept it. It wasn't that I didn't belong at Knox; it was that I wasn't a professor who, at that moment, could make learning accessible, rewarding, or kind. I was scraping together lectures at the last minute, refusing to give my students a little grace or breathing room or even a little time to figure out what history was about. I was unflinching in holding the line against what I perceived to be rampant absenteeism. I denied that my students or I needed anything but unshakable deadlines and an expectation that everyone would do the reading solely because I had written it on the syllabus. I didn't trust my students, which made all our lives harder than they needed to be. I stood in need of creative thought about disability, as so many of my students did too. And yet all I knew to do in the midst of this maelstrom was to plow on.

I wasn't completely ignorant of the fact that my classes weren't working as I wanted them to—that students weren't discussing ideas with me or each other, that they were struggling with the reading load, and that I loathed everything about lectures. After that first term I began to change things little by little. I picked different readings that were more accessible than the books I'd read in graduate school, and I made sure to prep for class earlier than I had before so that I felt confident giving up the control necessary to allow space for a discussion to take place. I experimented with reading journals, tried to give students more choice in how they fulfilled assignments, and got rid of the book reviews, which were as tedious to grade as I'm sure they were to write. This was often an isolating experience for me, as it is for so many of us who are launched, untrained, into academic careers.

But three things radically changed my pedagogy. The first was working with Elise Fillpot and an incredible group of K–12 schoolteachers in Iowa through Bringing History Home, a program funded by three Teaching American History grants from the U.S. Department of Education. From 2001 to 2011 we worked to change the way history was taught in schools—to have teachers help students focus on historical skills in the classroom by analyzing primary and secondary sources, using maps for geographic and other forms of knowledge, building timelines, and producing syntheses of everything they had learned. We knew that students as young as kindergarten could *be* historians, not just hear from them.[4]

Every one of the master teachers who helped lead the program was surpassingly kind—to me, to each other, to the teachers who attended our workshops, and to their students. They patiently walked me through the particular challenges of teaching history in K–5, where the state required very little in the way of social studies, and demonstrated how, with a little creativity, it could show up in math lessons (create a 3D map of downtown, for example) or in read-alouds of books with historical themes. They treated each other with enormous compassion and respect, forming a real community around teaching others the skills they already knew.

I learned from them and tore apart my terrible lecture-only class. While I kept a textbook as backup for students who might need extra reinforcement of what we were doing in the course, I built every class period around primary sources. My students and I borrowed the process of SOCC (Source, Observe, Contextualize, and Corroborate) from Bringing History Home and used it to analyze the documents and images with which we worked.[5] We worked in pairs and small groups; we made posters and timelines; we drew elaborate historical family trees; we wrote letters to the editors of newspapers from the 1820s. In short, I stopped talking, and my students filled that space with questions and comments—and thrived.

My second schooling in kindness came in June 2013 when I went to a four-day workshop in Ann Arbor, Michigan, to learn about the practice of Intergroup Dialogue with five Knox colleagues: Gabrielle Raley-Karlin, faculty from Anthropology-Sociology; Tianna Cervantez, the head of Multicultural Student Advisement; and three students: Maricruz Osario, Devin Hanley, and ChanTareya Paredes. Led by the staff and faculty of the Program on Intergroup Relations at the University of Michigan, the workshop focused on Dialogue as a long-standing, deeply researched approach to talking about oppression. Dialogue focuses on small-group interactions where members of different social groups engage in structured conversations to reach an understanding of oppression and privilege. An experiential form of learning, Dialogue asks participants think critically about their own and others' socialization into systems of power by talking frankly about personal experience.[6] It was an intense workshop, not simply because we were learning about the process, but because we were engaging in the process. Everyone had to participate in Dialogue every morning and every afternoon, and it was unlike anything I had experienced before.

Dialogue demands vulnerability. It wants to know how you feel, not just what you think, and for you to actively pull down the walls that we all build, day by day, between us and a full understanding of the consequences of our actions. A Dialogue circle is a place where you risk trust very quickly, and where hard truths are told. It's also a place where you do not try and fix things for people, comfort them, or offer them advice but simply hold space for them to encounter the totality of their thoughts and feelings. Dialogue is hard, hard work, but it can be transformational.

My colleagues and I agreed that our campus would benefit from a Dialogue program, and over the next several years we set about building one. But Dialogue has a habit of spilling out of Dialogue classes and into everything else you do. I realized that I had, for years, been asking my students to be vulnerable in class in everything from first-day introductions to end-of-term presentations, and yet I did not reciprocate. It felt important that I allow students to see something other than (a desperate approximation of) perfection and authority in my presence. I needed to ease up. I needed to think deeply about the social identities of my students and myself and design my teaching to meet us in the complex, messy places we inhabited. I needed to completely let go of the educator I had been taught to be in grad school and start over.

I would be remiss if I did not pause here to credit my colleague, Gabrielle Raley-Karlin, with facilitating so much of my growth in those wobbly years. We directed the Dialogue program on campus together and co-taught the facilitator training course every year. I was, at the beginning, still wedded to the idea that treating students equally was the way to be fair to everyone—that everyone should produce the same kind of work (usually written), and that everyone should turn things in on the same day and incur a penalty if they didn't. Gabe insisted I embrace equity instead and take into consideration the widely divergent experiences of our students in and out of the classroom, all of which shaped the work they produced. Gabe also pushed me to expand my understanding of disability, to learn more about what it meant to be neurodivergent and what it meant to teach with a ready abundance of grace. She also helped me see my own disabilities not as a badly dealt hand, or a nuisance, or an incumbrance, but as a part of me that I should embrace without apology.[7]

Third, while all of these largely professional developments were unfolding, I was doggedly working to recover from more than one experience of sexual violence. My first therapist in my new hometown left the state for a new position only six months after we started working together, but those six months were deeply meaningful. I showed up in Dr. Deborah Zera's office depressed, closed off, brittle, scared, and without a glimmer of understanding that I had PTSD. The diagnosis changed everything: once I had an explanatory framework for the dizzying range of symptoms I was experiencing, I felt incredible relief. Relief did not mean immediate recovery, but understanding what was happening to me helped me regain a sense of control over my life.

I vividly remember one evening session when I felt an overwhelming "thing." It was an emotion, although I don't remember which emotion it was and may not have known: distinguishing one feeling from another was a skill I had to learn. But I do remember shaking with fear just contemplating this amorphous "thing" I felt, and I couldn't believe Dr. Zera when she asked me to sit with it for two minutes. She told me she would keep time and that she would ensure nothing terrible would happen while I sat on the couch in her office and paid attention to the maelstrom inside me. Those two minutes were both excruciating and liberating. I learned to occupy my trembling body with patience, to catalog the aches and pains of my brain rejecting any challenge to its now-faulty defenses. I learned that my feelings would not actually demolish me and that I could tolerate two minutes of discomfort at a time. This was, Dr. Zera explained, the beginning of mindfulness, a compassionate path toward change.

Over the next several years I made a practice out of sitting (uneasily) with discomfort. I turned to the wisdom of different Buddhist traditions to teach me how to exist with my own pain and to greet the tumultuous outpouring of my stored-up emotions with kindness.[8] I learned to name my feelings, and then to greet them, and after many years to thank them for showing up. I discovered that meditation was not about the presence of an empty mind but about bringing compassion to bear on my twirling thoughts, observing them as a curiosity, and returning to the steadying rhythm of my breath. I am still very far from an expert at any of this; I'm a practitioner in that meditation takes a heck of a lot of practice. But engaging in that practice showed me that all sorts of kindness could act as a key to open the doors I'd kept stubbornly locked. I discovered that, after everything I had been through, it was, in the words of Naomi Shihab Nye, "only kindness that makes sense anymore."[9]

All of these threads of self-discovery, experimentation, and instruction came to a head in 2017 when, a full twenty-three years into a teaching career I was by then pretty proud of, I went to the Digital Pedagogy Lab at the University of Mary Washington. The entire institute was predicated upon the concept of kindness. From the pronoun buttons available at the registration desk, to the probing questions of the session leaders, to the time people took, one-on-one, to talk about syllabi and assignments, there was an ethos of care running through the whole four days of my residency. I had signed up for the Intro track and had expected to spend my time evaluating digital tools to bring into my classroom (a process in which I felt I was running sorely behind). I certainly had the opportunity to do that, but first I was asked to think about why I needed those tools at all and whom they would serve.

My fellow attendees and I were constantly asked to consider why we were doing things the way we were and what subtextual messages we were sending to our students about who *they* were. These questions were a revelation to me. I took a good long look at my syllabus and realized that, despite all the work I had done over the years to be flexible, creative, and inventive, and even to generate fun in the classroom, that document communicated nothing about those values. I wrote everything from a position of unassailable authority. The language I used to describe the Knox College honor code clearly conveyed the suspicion that everyone was going to commit some awful academic offense, while my attendance policy made no room for the idea that my students were adults with complicated lives who would need to miss a class now and again.[10] I had phrased everything in terms of things I would impart to my students from some mystical pedestal rather than—as I truly believed we should—discovering things together.

Why? Why did I posit my students as passive novices who couldn't contribute to their own learning? Why did I require students to jump through hoops to prove that they deserved an extension on a paper? Why did I dock points if my students missed three classes in a term? I couldn't articulate it at the time: I was still too ignorant of so much of my privilege and I lacked the language I needed. But I was beginning to see the reach of kyriarchy, the interlocking systems of oppression that shape who does and does not have power in the United States, and what forms of personal, communal, institutional, or systemic power are coded by a small number of powerful, rich, able-bodied, usually white men to be acceptable or even laudable in that society.[11] I was also seeing with new eyes the extent of my complicity in harmful, even lethal systems of hegemony. It was not just that I was, individually, choosing to cling to a form of authoritarianism in the classroom; it was that my actions represented a small cog in the enormous machine of colonialism, racism, queerphobia, misogyny, and ableism that harmed so many people.[12] That particular session at the Digital Pedagogy Lab was the first time I had been asked so bluntly to defend my pedagogical choices, and once I reflected, I found much of my pedagogy indefensible. At the time I felt regret and no small amount of embarrassment. My teaching was undone by the presence of a question that was never articulated quite this directly but was everywhere around me:

Why not be kind?

A pedagogy of kindness begins with justice. It's not possible to teach with compassion unless we first give critical thought to who is in our classroom, why, and what obstacles they might be facing. Many of us assume things about our students that don't hold up to scrutiny. Take the students featured in the (bad) advice handed down to me in graduate school: they were a vast monolith. They were all eighteen to twenty-two years old, white, living close to (if not on) campus, and neurotypical. They had food, cars, parents who paid for their education, terrible drinking habits, and a fascination with football. Some were athletes, and athletes were the worst offenders when it came to cheating. They were straight, Christian, and likely a member of a campus sorority or fraternity. They were also a myth.

Today's college students do not fit the monolithic description of that eighteen-to-twenty-two-year-old, if they ever did. While there are institutions where some or all of these experiences might ring true, there are far more where the student body defies these categorizations. As many as 71 percent of undergraduate students in the United States are nontraditional, defined by higher education administrator Kris MacDonald as students who are "at least 25 years old, attend school part-time, work full-time . . . a veteran, have children, wait at least one year after high school before entering college, have a GED instead of a high school diploma . . . [are] a first-generation student (FGS), are enrolled in nondegree programs, or have reentered a college program."[13] As of the 2015–16 academic year, approximately 45 percent of undergraduate students were students of color (up from 30 percent ten years earlier), of which 0.4 percent were Native students.[14] According to the American College Health Association, 20 percent of college students in 2019 identified as LGBTQIA,[15] and—taking into account the number of students who may feel unsafe reporting on their sexuality or gender identity to people in positions of power—the actual proportion of LGBTQIA students is likely higher. The National Center for Education Statistics records that in the 2015–16 academic year, 19 percent of undergraduates in the United States reported having a disability.[16] In its #Real College Survey in 2021, the Hope Center for Community, College, and Justice found that 52 percent of responding students at two-year colleges and 43 percent of students at four-year colleges had experienced housing insecurity. Thirty-nine percent of responding students at two-year colleges and 29 percent of students at four-year colleges had faced insecurity related to food.[17]

This is just a sampling of how diverse our student bodies are overall. Many institutions, such as historically Black colleges and universities (HBCUs), Hispanic-serving institutions (HSIs), tribal colleges, women's colleges, and community colleges serve student bodies that have different social demographics based on axes of class, race, gender, sexuality, and more. It's worth asking about the specific makeup of the student body at your institution and where information is lacking and your position is secure enough to press for change, asking for answers to questions like "How many of our students are hungry?" At heart, we shouldn't make assumptions about who our students are but rather make it a point to get to know them—demographically and otherwise. All our other efforts will flounder if we cannot attend to the basic issues of economic, racial, social, and cultural injustice that permeate our campuses. Compassion asks who is in the room, who is not, and why they are or are not there. Niceness does not.[18]

A pedagogy of kindness is also a practice of believing students. When a student comes to me to say that their grandparent died, I believe them. When they email me to say they have the flu, I believe them. When they tell me they didn't have time to read, I believe them. When they tell me their printer failed, I believe them. There's an obvious chance that I could be taken advantage of in this scenario, that someone could straight-up lie and get away with it. But I've learned that I would rather take that risk, and deal with exceptions as they arise, than make life more difficult for my students struggling with grief and illness or even an overpacked schedule or faulty electronics. It costs me nothing to be kind, and the results have been transformative for everyone in our shared classroom space. Students have not, en masse, started refusing to meet deadlines, but the students who are struggling have had time to finish their work. Students have not, en masse, started skipping class, but they're not required to undergo the invasive act of telling me personal details about their lives when they can't show up. Students have not, en masse, started doubting my abilities or my expertise, but they have stepped forward to direct their own education in meaningful and exciting ways that I could not have thought of. The entire process of teaching has become immeasurably more fun.

We should believe students, and we should believe *in* students. Believing in students means seeing them as collaborators—believing they have valuable contributions to make to the way in which syllabi, assignments, and assessments are designed, and life experiences that should be respected in the classroom. This has changed everything for me, not simply in terms of my thinking, but in terms of concrete acts within my classroom. I design assignments differently, grade differently, think hard about flexibility and choice, and fundamentally do not approach my students' disabilities (or my own) as representing the lack of something but rather the positive presence of so much.

Kindness is a discipline. We will not always *feel* like being compassionate, especially when we're frustrated by the circumstances of our employment, be that shaped by administrative decisions with which we disagree, precarity, or a day when nothing in our classroom goes the way we planned. We have lives beyond the classroom too. We weather grief, we worry about our finances, we create families, we support our friends. Whether colored by joy or marred by despair, our lives demand our attention—and sometimes leave us with little left to give to others. That's when, more than ever, we need to pause before replying to a student's email, or take a breath before opening our door for student hours, or consider our options for a moment while on the bus, on the train, or in our car before we gird our loins and start the day. We do not need to direct our energy into niceness. Instead, we need to remind ourselves that we believe in compassion and act upon that belief, even on the days when we are spitting mad, hollowed out, and heartsore.

I feel more comfortable as a teacher now than I ever have. The subconscious sense that students were antagonists lingered inside me for a long time—long enough that it is still a wonder to teach and to experience a teacher-student relationship that lacks that default expectation. I am less stressed, and I no longer have reservations about walking into the classroom.[19] My students rise up to meet every new challenge I present to them. It seems that the practice has been transformational for them and for me.

In the fall of 2019, I taught a brand-new course on history pedagogy. Acutely aware of how little preparation graduate students in history receive before they are asked to teach, I decided to create a class that would give students the opportunity to think about pedagogy before they faced their first classroom full of undergraduates. Students interested in history from our elementary and secondary education programs also joined the course. Together, we thought about skills that are central to historical inquiry: analyzing primary and secondary sources, using maps, creating timelines, building context, and producing synthesis. But we also spent a lot of time thinking about kindness—about the type of teacher that each of them wanted to be, and the ways they could do that within the restrictions and limitations placed upon them by schools and graduate programs.

At the end of term, students had the opportunity to appraise the class through an anonymous online evaluation tool. Beyond the college's standard queries asked about every class on campus, each student in the class responded to the question I had added: What was the most important thing you learned this term? Here are four of the answers (all of them are available upon request):

> The education system needs to change and it is up to the participants of that system to change it for the better.
> Just how important knowing yourself is to the process of creating a teaching philosophy and pedagogy.
> I've learned that kindness should extend to every part of your life, and education is not an exception. Instead, education is maybe one of the most important places to implement kindness towards others as a philosophy and lifestyle.
> The most important thing I've learned this term is to be yourself when you teach. You don't have to conform to what certain people say. Also teach with kindness and an open heart. Truly believe in your students. And that is what I feel Cate does with us.[20]

A pedagogy of kindness is within our collective reach. We're all trying, I believe, to make a real difference in our students' lives and to provide them the tools and the knowledge to make wise choices as they move beyond the classroom and into new lines of work or study. I've written this book as an invitation, an opportunity to accompany me on the pedagogical evolution I've been (and still am) going through, and to consider adding kindness to the repertoire of thinking, doing, and reflecting that makes up a teaching life. Change is not just possible but meaningful and good. I haven't always taught well, but I take real joy in discovering how to be a better teacher by being in a compassionate relationship with my students and by honoring their humanity in the things that we do.

In this book you'll find ideas for how to approach your own pedagogy, and your own students, with kindness. You'll also find advice, where appropriate, for extending kindness to yourself. Remember, as with any new tool, you don't need to do everything in a single day. Take a couple of these ideas and weave them into your own classroom practice. Blend them with the commitments you already have. Change part of your syllabus if changing everything seems too much (or if there is language that your institution mandates that you include). Carve out ten minutes for yourself if twenty or thirty feels impossible. Adapt these suggestions so that they speak to who you are as an educator and human being.

Kindness is not a destination but a practice and a journey. I am not writing from some pinnacle of enlightenment; I am learning every day how to show up for myself and my students in the most authentic, open, trusting, and compassionate ways I can. I hope this book will suggest ways in which we might collectively do this, and offer practical tips to transform what might feel like an airy philosophy into concrete action. I write as a white, full professor at a small liberal arts college in a rural area, and your experiences may be very different to mine. You are the authority on yourself and your classroom. But I hope that together we can create bright new spaces, rooted in compassion, in which all of us engaged in teaching and learning will thrive.

1

KINDNESS TOWARD
THE SELF

For all the differences between us, instructors in higher ed commonly share a defining experience: there is more work in the day than there are hours to do it. There is a real difference between working at a major research institution with the protections of tenure and piecing together an income from adjunct positions at multiple schools. All but a handful of us must navigate grave inequities of compensation, benefits, access, reward, and respect, depending on where we work and how others perceive our abilities. Yet, whether the pressure placed on us is to grade two hundred exams over a weekend, or to serve on multiple committees when our colleagues serve on one, or to produce a piece of scholarship that will provide us with something like job security, there are few among us who would claim to have time enough to do it.

To be asked to spend time with our pedagogy, to expand our awareness of the scholarship of teaching and learning, to rethink our practices, and to design anew can therefore feel like a momentous ask. We work hard, and it's not as if our jobs represent the totality of our lives. We have family responsibilities, kinship duties, friendships to nourish, dogs to walk, groceries to buy, our health to care for, and laundry to be done. We have social lives; we have films to watch and TV shows to escape to; we volunteer; we are activists; we are fond of novels and comics and audiobooks; the lawn needs mowing, and some of us must shovel the snow. Where, in all of this, can we find the time to think structurally about pedagogical kindness? How is this not just one more thing to do?

Kindness is not a practice that appears in a vacuum. If we want to be kind to others, to create classroom experiences that are alive with compassion for everyone involved, we have to start by being kind to ourselves. The idea can seem trite, a nod toward the convoluted concept of self-care, which, in its most lackluster formulation, has come to mean taking bubble baths or drinking a good cup of tea. In the words of Yamiko Marama, "For the longest time our consumer-driven society has been able to individualise, commodify, de-politicise and commercialise self-care. We've distorted it so much, we're not sure what it means outside of Instagram influencers and Lululemon active wear."[1]

But it is worth considering what self-care can and should mean. While I raise the concept here in relation to teaching, self-care cannot be a practice (or series of practices) that is solely concerned with supporting work. To practice self-care to simply be better at or more available to our jobs is a profoundly limited vision, albeit one that has popular currency.[2] That kind of care exists in service to capitalism, with all its attendant flaws, and rarely in service to each of us as whole human beings with lives that expand beyond the reaches of our jobs. Caring for ourselves is about securing the time, energy, creativity, and rest we need to support our existence in all its wonderful, frustrating, liberating complexity. Many people love the profession of education and derive tremendous satisfaction and affirmation from working in this field. But even then we must remember we are all so much more than the work that we do.

To care is, according to philosopher Nel Noddings, to enter into a relationship: someone cares for someone, and someone else acknowledges that care. Caring looks different for different people, in different situations, and under different circumstances. "To care is to act not by fixed rule but by affection and regard," Noddings writes. Caring is "varied rather than rule-bound; that is . . . [someone's caring] actions, while predictable in a global sense, will be unpredictable in detail."[3] While it's pretty easy to imagine what this looks like when the person doing the caring and the person being cared for are different people, it's perhaps harder to conceptualize when we think about ourselves. But self-care runs along much the same lines, although the relationship is not between two people but between ourselves-in-the-now and ourselves-in-the-future. When we act with care toward ourselves, we act in our holistic best interest so that our future self will appreciate what we've done. It is self-care, for example, to acknowledge the material circumstances of my body, to understand that I need fuel to live my life: food, rest, and things that stimulate my mind. It is self-care to acknowledge my need for connection: family, perhaps, or partnerships, or friendships, or communities that strengthen and support me. It is self-care to seek out these things, and it is self-care to want to grow.

Yet we do not exist as isolated individuals but inside societies and cultures that send us messages about the degree to which others think we are deserving of care. Our access to care—even self-care—is knowingly limited by people who understand their privileges to be dependent upon denying others the material, emotional, social, and spiritual space they need. In the academy this is reflected in matters like the move to contingency; in the loss of lines in departments and programs that ask hard questions about equity and inclusion (like gender and women's studies, Latinx studies, and African American studies); and in the tolerance of sexual harassment, abuse, and assault.[4] The academy is also far from insulated from events beyond our physical and virtual campuses, such as continuing police brutality toward Black people, Indigenous people, and people of color, the denial of asylum at our borders, and the persistence of anti-Semitism and Islamophobia.[5] Indeed, the academy is oftentimes the institution doling out that harm. Those in a position to make changes to the policies and systems that produce such violence rarely do so, communicating a fundamental lack of care for the basic safety and well-being of too many among us. We carry this with us every day.[6]

This makes self-care a profoundly political act, one that is for so many of us "not self-indulgence, but . . . self-preservation," as Audre Lorde put it in 1988. Lorde's words have often been quoted to define the necessity of self-care, but it is crucial to recognize that she spoke not in general terms but as a Black lesbian feminist living with cancer. Her words are, as Jina B. King and Sami Schalk write, inseparable from "a radical politics of self-care . . . inextricably tied to the lived experiences and temporalities of multiply marginalized people, especially disabled queer people, disabled people of color, and disabled queer people of color."[7] Self-care in these terms is very far from the act of buying new nail polish or sipping a glass of wine. "I do not find it difficult to spoil myself," writes Marama. "I'm good at consuming—whatever form it happens to be. . . . All of these things feel good for a time. However, these activities never leave me healed."[8]

We badly need a vision and practice of self-care that heals, especially in academia—especially in an academia that continues to be hostile to so many of us along axes of race, gender, sexuality, religion, nationality, citizenship, disability, and class. We need a self-care that shouts when fields run *too fast*, demanding fealty to accelerating timetables of achievement, requiring that we prove our worth based on a handful of narrowly identified artifacts.[9] We need a self-care that allows us to sustainably make demands of our institutions, demands that place our well-being at the center of everyday operations, strategic planning, and crisis response. We need a self-care that is not complicit in circumstances that create suffering for others. We do need, in Noddings's words, affection and regard, but we need those concepts applied in their broadest, most political sense. We need to pause, and to breathe, and to be truthful about the academy in which we work.[10]

And where is kindness in this? Kindness toward the self, I would suggest, refines the idea of self-care to make space for reconciliation, forgiveness, and accountability. Kindness asks us to approach ourselves with Noddings's regard and reconcile our sense of self with the places where we feel we did not measure up on any given day. Kindness understands our imperfections, frailties, and the things we don't know, and suggests that we cannot move forward in the world without the opportunity to pardon ourselves for our mistakes. But kindness also holds us accountable; it does not suggest we "let things go" without examining them, considering our positionality, and assimilating that knowledge into our understanding of who we are, what we prioritize, and where we must try again. To dismiss the places where we trip in word, thought, or action without reflecting on the impact of each is nothing more than being nice, relieving ourselves of responsibility and prioritizing feeling good over being just. To provide a concrete example of this in action: in the Social Justice Dialogues courses on the Knox campus, we use a set of ground rules for conversation adapted from those created by the Program on Intergroup Relations at the University of Michigan. One of those ground rules is "We will remember that all of us have learned misinformation about ourselves, our social groups, and other social groups. Discrimination functions, in part, by keeping us uninformed. We will not blame ourselves or others for getting something wrong on the first try. After we have learned new information, however, we will hold ourselves and others accountable for that information." It is a rule which offers the mix of reconciliation, forgiveness, and accountability that is central to being kind.[11]

These ideas are still somewhat abstract: they do not necessarily tell us how to find space within the overwhelming press of our working lives as we try and get through graduate school, pay the bills, secure benefits, get a permanent job, get our contract renewed, make tenure, manage our load, and teach. We manage our work lives within structures and institutions that exert a tremendous amount of pressure on the way we do our jobs. We have agency, but that agency is not as simple as trying to time-manage our way out of this collective mess. This is because behind every time management tip is an existential problem, suggests writer Oliver Burkeman: we have a finite amount of time on this earth. We spend inordinate energy trying to avoid this reality and chasing down the perfect "someday" when we will achieve peace, satisfaction, and inbox zero. Life—especially our work life—appears to us like a puzzle. "Perhaps you're familiar with the extraordinarily irritating parable of the rocks in the jar," Burkeman writes:

> In the version with which I'm most familiar, a teacher arrives in class one day carrying several sizable rocks, some pebbles, a bag of sand, and a large glass jar. He issues a challenge to his students: Can they fit all the rocks, pebbles, and sand into the jar? The students . . . try putting the pebbles or the sand in first, only to find that the rocks won't fit. Eventually—and no doubt with a condescending smile—the teacher demonstrates the solution: he puts the rocks in first, then the pebbles, then the sand, so that the smaller items nestle comfortably in the spaces between the larger ones. The moral is that if you make time for the most important things first, you'll get them all done and have plenty of room for less important things besides.

As Burkeman explains, this parable falls apart as soon as you take into account the fact that the teacher selected exactly how many rocks, pebbles, and bags of sand to give the students. The teacher did not bring in all the rocks in the world, and if he had done so, the students would have had to simply agree to leave some rocks out. That's the real heart of the story, Burkeman writes. We cannot get all the rocks in the jar; we have to drop a lot of rocks in life, and we have to be okay with it.[12]

Knowing Ourselves

How much preparation each of us has had to become a teacher by the time we walk into a classroom for the first time varies wildly by program and place and is deeply bound up with questions of compassion. Many professors training graduate students do not believe it is necessary to train individuals in pedagogy; some believe that a limited amount of training—rather than an actual course of study—is enough; still other programs provide deeper engagement with issues of instruction.[13] These varied experiences have a profound effect on our sense of self as we enter the classroom. There is much here that needs to be addressed at the institutional and structural level. It is manifestly unjust to place individuals in classrooms without proper training in the pedagogy of their field and, more generally, our best understanding of how humans learn. Yet this happens all the time. Being a student and having experienced other people's teaching does not directly translate into an individual knowing how to teach, even if their role models are accomplished instructors. This is too often how teaching careers in higher education begin.

Take the lecture, my own fallback position when I first started out as an assistant professor. There is clear research that long lectures, without breaks for questions from students or interactive activities of any kind, don't make space for students to learn as well as they do when we apply active-learning strategies, even if students themselves enjoy the lecture format. Yet most universities run on lectures. Intro classes are often several hundred students strong in large research universities, and that makes active learning daunting. With pressure on all fields to maintain or even increase enrollment, there's also little incentive for departments to change the structure of how introductory courses are taught. Professors have often been educated primarily through lectures and figure they did okay under those conditions, forgetting that—as people setting out on the road to being a professor whether they knew it at the time or not—they were probably one of a handful of students who found the subject—not to mention the ability to focus for an extended period of time—easy. To many graduate students, lectures can seem like a milestone achievement, a reflection of the sizable content they've learned. Without intervention, without critical consideration of pedagogical research and what it means for how we approach our students, this pattern can effectively mean "rinse and repeat" forever. We do what we know how to do under the circumstances in which we're employed, and that does not always serve us or our students well.[14]

There are some people who can intuit how to teach. They do not make up the majority of educators, and there's not one lick of shame in that for the rest of us. Just as we study in our fields of interest for years to absorb massive quantities of content and produce original work, it follows that we should read and study and practice to become good teachers. This means that those of us with security and seniority should be advocating for pedagogical training and support for our most junior department members, be they graduate students or early-career faculty. It also means we should enthusiastically support the work of educators working in teaching and learning centers on our campuses, and seek out opportunities for consistent professional development. So many instructors have terrible dreams about teaching, about being unprepared, unable to manage a classroom environment, or ignored by their students. These situations are ones of high anxiety, even when only in thought. Our responsibility toward one another is to make sure these experiences are not the stuff of reality and to mutually assure each other's success.

Many educators worry that they are inadequate.[15] We worry that we don't know enough (about either our subject matter or teaching); we worry about the choices we have or haven't made about course materials and assignments; we worry that we'll be taken advantage of; we worry about our position vis-à-vis our students. What's our authority? Do we want to *be* an authority? What presumptions do our students carry about our race, sexuality, gender, class, disabilities, and religious beliefs that might complicate these questions even further?[16] We worry that our students will know we feel nervous or afraid—even more, that they won't respect us.

Respect is both earned and a reciprocal process: we should expect that it will not be as developed on day one as on the last day of the course. Yet beyond this is the fact that many students (and colleagues) have absorbed or even purposefully cultivated gross misinformation about their own social identities and that of other people.[17] They may act upon that misinformation, challenging BIPOC and LGBTQIA educators as well as those from religious backgrounds or economic classes different to their own, as well as teachers with disabilities. The pressure to be overprepared as a condition of entering the classroom, to dress "professionally," and to police our speech cannot be overstated, especially when, as Jesica Siham Fernández explores in "Critical Reflexivity as a Tool for Students," the "quotidian image of the professor most students will describe . . . is someone who is a White male in their late fifties, who wears glasses and tweed suits. The professor is also someone with an impersonal, straightforward attitude." Whether or not we ourselves feel obligated to approximate this ideal, we are part of the social body of our institutions, which means we are all implicated in addressing the gap between this presumption and the lived realities of our lives. We need not to only honor our colleagues' choices in dress, honorifics, and demeanor but to consider if our own ease—if we have it—comes at a cost to others.[18]

Our confidence in our ability to teach, and to create a classroom space in which respect flourishes, is also bound up with our understanding of our own positionality. We cannot be good teachers and live unexamined lives. Anyone who has experienced oppression knows where they stand in relation to those who would oppress them. I have, for example, spent my life learning how to live in a patriarchy as a cisgender woman; how to dodge, weave, protect, and recover from passive as well as active ideas and acts that would harm me. But it is often far harder for us to acknowledge where we hold privilege—the places where we accrue unearned social benefits because of some part of where we were born, to whom, and under what circumstances. Our experiences of oppression and privilege can separate us from our students, and theirs can separate them from us, without us centering our attention on the question of what contributes to making us who we are.

I did not fully consider the ramifications of my social identities in the classroom until 2013. Before that, I understood the instances where I should anticipate being the target of someone's derision, blame, or hostility when I was in a position of lesser social power; I knew that because of sexism—including that internalized by other women—students tended to rate men in the professoriate as more competent and better at their jobs than women, for example.[19] But I had not wrestled with my privileges nearly enough. I hadn't considered that I benefited from speaking English as my first language, for example, or that my British accent was considered fun by students while my colleagues from other nations found themselves stigmatized for speaking with inflection. My understanding of my whiteness was too superficial; I probably would have identified as "one of the good ones" if challenged. And while I was a first-gen student, born and raised working-class, I hadn't wrestled with the fact that my U.S. class status was shifting as I gained more and more education.

One of the first things my colleagues and I did at the 2013 National Intergroup Dialogue Institute was fill out a social identity wheel.[20] The exercise asked us to put together a composite picture of ourselves through our social identities—identities that made us part of particular social groups by virtue of things like our race, class, and gender. We were asked to consider which identities we considered most often. Those, our breakout-group leaders suggested, were usually where we were targeted for oppression; they stuck out to us because we were constantly being harassed or harmed in those places.[21] Our group leaders then asked us to consider which identities we thought about *least* often. Those were the spots where we usually possessed privilege—the privilege not to think about that part of our identity because it had been socially labeled as normal.

We were also asked to consider which of our identities we wanted to know more about. On the surface, the question seemed facile: each of these identities helped make us who we were, so surely we were familiar with their contours. But under the least bit of scrutiny it became clear that—most especially where each of us was privileged—we had given very little consideration to how that identity impacted others as we moved through the world. We were invited to start educating ourselves and were supplied with readings to help us make that shift. These questions—this invitation—changed the way I thought about myself and my classroom forever.

Below is a social identity reflection chart. It is adapted from that first social identity wheel to which my colleagues and I were introduced in Michigan in 2013 and which came from a program at Arizona State University that is no longer in operation. My colleague Gabrielle Raley-Karlin and I have since added a couple of categories that frequently came up as we did this exercise with students, and we learned to create a "more" category for group memberships that we had not anticipated.

Consider filling out the chart. This is an exercise that's solely for yourself; you need not share the results with anyone. Use as many words as necessary to explain your identity in ways that resonate with your experiences. Sometimes one-word answers suffice, and sometimes we need whole paragraphs to explain the complexity of belonging. Once you're done, ask yourself the same questions my colleagues and I were asked back in 2013: Which identities do you think about most, where you are

TABLE 1   Social Identity Reflection

Identity	Reflection
Race	
Ethnicity	
Nationality/Citizenship	
Indigenous Affiliation/Citizenship	
First Language	
Class	
Gender	
Sexuality	
Religion/Spirituality	
Age	
Disabilities	
Other:	

Source: Adapted by Catherine Denial and Gabrielle Raley-Karlin from the Social Identity Wheel, created by the Intergroup Relations Center at Arizona State University.

likely to be experiencing oppression, and which identities do you think about least, where you are likely to be experiencing privilege? Consider freewriting or recording a voice memo of your reflection.

Once you've considered how these identities show up in your life, consider how they show up in your classroom, broadly understood. How do they shape your assumptions about who you should or must be in that space? How does that have an impact upon the sorts of relationships you're able to build with your students? Where are you likely to experience pain when someone pokes one of your identities particularly hard? How can you anticipate that and build reflection, support, and care into your preparation for and experience of being an educator? Where do you need to learn more about certain identities and how they intersect with the identities of other people? How might you begin that work? This is the labor that undergirds our ability to be kind.

As we find and build the structures of care we need to flourish, it's important that we take individual steps to make our semiconscious worries visible or audible to ourselves as we establish mental, emotional, and physical spaciousness for ourselves. We can take inventory of everything that worries us as we contemplate teaching. We can write a list on our phones, use a tried-and-true piece of paper and a pencil, or record a voice memo. We can express what we're feeling in words or in symbols or doodles. The medium is not as important as the act of facing everything spinning around in our minds. This can, without question, be an overwhelming task in and of itself that we'd sometimes rather avoid; we're often afraid that seeing or hearing all these thoughts at the same time will overwhelm us further. My experience has been that seeing everything on my list helps make it more manageable, a concrete thing I can tackle as opposed to free-range thoughts running amok. But if you feel like making a list is too much, move on to the step below and simply address each thought as it pops into your mind over time.

With list in hand (or ear), focus on each item, pretending that the fears were expressed by a dear friend who is nervous about entering the classroom. Approach each element with kindness. If your friend needed counsel, what advice would you give them? Below, I offer a sampling of the worries I have experienced in the past—a short list of fears drawn from my own teaching life to suggest what this might look like:

- *I'm worried I'll trip, spill coffee down my shirt, write on the white-board with a permanent marker, be unable to get the technology to work, or do something else that will be profoundly embarrassing.*

All of these things will happen to you at some point in your teaching career. They are accidents. They will not imprint in your students' minds as the only thing worth remembering about you. Carry a stain remover wipe and the contact information for whoever takes care of the tech in your classroom, and remember that if you write over permanent marker with an erasable one, both can be wiped off the board.

• *I don't know enough about this subject.*
Even the most privileged professors, with the most time to keep up with their field, don't know everything about their subject. Indeed, it's a truism that the longer you teach, the more you understand you don't know. Start small; make sure you've read the texts one week ahead of your students, for example. And don't be afraid to say "I don't know" and "I'll get back to you with an answer." Acknowledging our limitations is better than bluffing. Demonstrate curiosity and show students you'll follow through on learning more.

• *I don't know enough about teaching.*
There is a basic matter of justice on the line here: no one should be sent into a classroom feeling like they have no idea what they should do. But no matter how much preparation you have or haven't had, you're likely to feel out of your depth when you begin. Remember that nothing is irrevocable. Show up ready to make changes piece by piece. As you gather more data over the duration of the semester, you can change course. Find good blogs, books, podcasts, and videos about teaching and try them on for size. Make one change and see how it goes. Be transparent with your students about the pedagogical reasons for what you're doing, and invite them into the reflective work of teaching with you.

Boundaries as the Bedrock of Kindness

Despite the things beyond our control in our teaching lives, there are times, practices, and strategies that we get to craft and, crucially, boundaries that we need to put in place and maintain if we want to be kind. We cannot lose sight of the enormous work ahead of us to make higher education welcoming, just, and achievable for everyone. But the things which we control are usually small; they're the incremental decisions that can shape a day where we can implement changes that have a meaningful impact upon both our well-being and the store of compassion we have to direct elsewhere. This is not an evasion of responsibility. As adrienne maree brown articulates in her book *Emergent Strategy*, "How we are at the small scale is how we are at the large scale. . . . Grace [Lee Boggs] articulated it in what might be the most-used quote of my life: '*Transform yourself to transform the world.*' This doesn't mean to get lost in the self, but rather to see our own lives and work and relationships as a front line, a first place we can practice justice, liberation, and alignment with each other and the planet."[22] Here are some concrete suggestions for showing kindness to the self.

1. Invest in your pedagogical development.

Some of my loneliest moments as an educator have been while trying to figure out what good teaching actually is. This applies to us whether we are graduate students and faculty stepping into a classroom early in our careers or seasoned instructors with decades of experience under our belts: we are never done learning about learning. New research about cognition, disability, inclusivity, and classroom practice is published all the time, and just as we keep abreast of developments in our disciplinary fields, it ought to be incumbent upon us to keep up with the scholarship of teaching and learning (SOTL) too. This may sound like one more thing we have to do when time is already short, but I would suggest that this work can make our lives easier rather than harder. My teaching is more effective, for example, because I seek out information about how my brain and my students' brains work. Learning about how communities form has also been vital to me, especially in an age of pandemic dislocation.

We need not go it alone in this venture. Almost every campus has a teaching and learning center; some have reading and writing labs, too—or at least a dedicated member of staff whose job it is to support our development as educators. If you're contingent, it's likely that it's hard to attend in-person, on-site workshops or talks, but there are freelance faculty developers offering courses and community in multiple modalities and at various times of the day. Do a Google search for online workshops—especially the ones that are free or low-cost—and check to see which journals in your discipline regularly feature teaching content. Sign up for the *Chronicle of Higher Education*'s weekly teaching newsletter to stay connected to new developments, debates, and ideas. It is a kindness to ourselves to grant that we all need help with teaching, a precursor to all the other work we do to compassionately manage our literal and figurative educational space.

2. Take time off from email.

The things that make email a blessing are also the things that make it a curse: it's accessible to us almost everywhere; it can be attended to at any hour of the day; and it allows for rapid communication with almost everyone with whom we work. Because of these things, email can quite easily expand like insulating foam to fill every nook and cranny of our lives. That's why it's so important to delineate boundaries around email and to teach our students and colleagues how and when we will respond.

There is no one-size-fits-all approach to limiting the time we spend on email. For me, it works to take most of the weekend off from checking my work email, but for some the weekend is prime working time. Some people devote an hour in the morning and an hour in the evening to handling email and noting those items that need more protracted attention. For others, the weight of the email waiting to be sorted in those hours feels burdensome, and attending to email as it arrives works better. Even then, setting aside twenty minutes every couple of hours to balance the need and desire to do other things while preventing email from becoming overwhelming is key. Whatever strategy works for you, cultivate time away from email and communicate your approach to others. I tell my students, on my syllabus and in person, that I rarely check email on weekends and that I log off around 8:00 p.m. on weeknights. I use my vacation setting to tell people when I'm unavailable and when I'll be able to reply to them again. I don't have push notifications on my phone for work emails, and I have colleagues who have removed their work email from their device entirely so that they cannot give in to the urge to check in just one more time at the grocery store or the concert or right before bed.

You might also consider scheduling your emails to send during the day, rather than at whatever hour of the morning, evening, or night you go through your inbox. This is a courtesy to others; it prevents people from feeling pressured to reply in times they may prefer to set aside for nonwork pursuits. But it is a kindness that pays dividends in modeling how you would like to be treated. If you hate dealing with emails that come in at 9:00 p.m., don't send them to others at that time. The feedback loop on this is imperfect, but it can make a meaningful difference to the way you think about what deserves your attention and when.

3. Take time off from work.

Time away from email is a game-changer when it comes to opening up space in our minds and bodies to think, create, and generate. Taking time away from work altogether is an even more necessary practice. We cannot consistently sustain singular thoughts and behaviors; our brains thrive on variation.[23] Time away from work is time that gives our brains the opportunity to turn thorny problems over in our minds until they unsnarl and new ideas come to fruition. But time away from work is not just about creating the conditions for better work. It has long been a demand of the labor movement that workers not only have a right to fair working conditions and compensation, but enough time, energy, and money for rest and rejuvenation, family and friends, and activities that replenish our sense of joy.[24]

Time off from work often feels difficult, because we are never short of lessons to plan, feedback to give, research to complete, writing to undertake, and administrative work to clear. Depending on the conditions of our employment, we may find it next to impossible because of the sheer number of courses we must string together to fulfill our contracted hours or stitch together an income. But to work without ceasing often results in diminishing returns. The more tired we become and the greater monotony of how we spend our time, the lesser the number and quality of the things we achieve. Put more simply, doing work for a long time is not the same as doing work well. This is a lesson we often try to impart to our incredibly busy students but don't always take to heart ourselves. Put downtime on your calendar. It is as important to schedule as the class periods when you teach.

4. Think creatively about your commute.

Commutes are often time-consuming and frustrating. We commute because we have to and not necessarily because we would choose to if there were greater equity in our compensation packages, the rent we pay, housing prices, and access to the transportation of our choice. Which is why it's so important to put our commutes on our daily calendars and to take them into account when assessing the amount of time and energy we have in a given day. Commuting takes energy, and no matter how we use the time—to read, to listen to music or podcasts, to pay bills on our phone, to stare into space and think—we arrive at our destinations having used up some of the finite store of self we have until we next get to rest. Award that expenditure of energy the recognition it deserves.

Some of us don't have a commute but instead work from home and teach online, and for those individuals a commute might be something to add. A commute in this sense does not mean traveling from home to a separate workplace but rather allowing there to be a transition between our work and nonwork lives. In the early months of the pandemic, I made tea and then lit a candle at my dining room table to delineate that space as my office and classroom. I would often listen to music that would allow me to focus or that helped me shift to a new frame of mind. These small rituals helped me feel I was leaving my "me" space and transitioning to a workspace, even if the two were realistically only a few feet apart.[25] Similarly, blowing out my candle was a concrete act that delineated the end of work time and the beginning of something new. It was a hard stop, a ritual that signified I was leaving work behind.

5. Schedule time for eating and rest.

In July 2021, I was diagnosed with type 2 diabetes, and it felt as if someone had placed my life in a snow globe, shaken it vigorously, and left me to figure out what to do next. One of the greatest challenges for the following year was learning not just what to eat so that I could be well but when to eat. The teaching days where I would subsist on string cheese, almonds, and mini–Snickers bars grabbed between classes were well and truly over. I was forced to start scheduling lunch breaks for myself. Eating to manage my illness meant taking time to cook and to pay attention to what I was consuming in a way that made concurrent meetings with colleagues and students impossible. If I didn't respect my body's need for food, I would at the very least be left with all the symptoms of low blood sugar—including the inability to generate a clear thought—and at worse would be putting myself at grave risk.

But it shouldn't have taken a diabetes diagnosis for me to recognize my basic humanity—to allow that all bodies need fuel, and that rest is a prerequisite for action. In addition, working through lunch (or coffee breaks or dinner) not only messes with our ability to get energy to our brains but signals our institutions' creep into spaces that we have an absolute right to reclaim. While many academics treasure the flexible work hours provided by the particular circumstances of their employment, this should not mean surrendering control over our basic needs. As journalist Anne Helen Petersen puts it in a meditation on the necessity of eating lunch, "More work does not necessarily make *better* work. There are diminishing returns to productivity culture, and work will expand to fill whatever parcel of time you give it. When you shorten the workday or the workweek—or mandate paid time off for rest and rejuvenation—you end up with workers who are more resilient, both intellectually and physically. Creativity, innovation, precision, perception—so many of the characters that are fundamental to a job well done—become elusive without resting the body and the mind."[26] Food, water, and rest matter. Put these things on your calendar and respect them as nonnegotiable commitments.

6. Build catch-up days into your courses.

It is a rare instructor who makes it through an entire semester without needing to perform acrobatics with class time. Whether we fall ill, or a lesson takes longer to execute than we had imagined, or our students ask many more questions than their predecessors did, learning has a habit of slopping out of its regularly scheduled hours and into others. We scramble—we merge lesson plans and cut activities and try to come up with newly efficient ways of communicating complex subjects. But how much easier if we simply built catch-up days into our semesters from the beginning?

Dedicate a class period or two on your syllabus to the work of catching up. The catch-up days in my courses are always used. Sometimes it's that we delve so deeply into a discussion that one class period cannot do the topic justice. Sometimes I'm sick, or it's −40°F with windchill (true story) and no one should be crossing campus in the snow. Sometimes world events take precedence over what's on the syllabus and it's important to provide time for my students and myself to process those things in community. At other moments, I realize I need to backtrack to clarify points that were unclear on another day. Sometimes the entire class needs a mental health day to reset, and sometimes I do too. Provide grace in your planning. Schedule breathing room, and as a bonus, let class go early once in a while.

7. Guard your yes.

For as long as I can remember in my academic life, friends and colleagues have exhorted me to say no: no to extra service, no to that book review request, no to staying late in my office, no to any number of actions that could (and did) lead to overwork. But saying no is hard, and it wasn't until I crossed paths with Beth Godbee and René Brooks that I learned a different approach to shaping my life—the power of a meaningful yes.

Godbee is an educator, a writer, and a coach with whom I've worked for several years, and I have benefited from her thoughtfulness, guidance, and questions related to writing and academia at large. In the spring of 2019, I burned out at my job—somewhat predictably, after going up for and earning a promotion—and it was with Godbee's help that I poked into all the nooks and crannies of my professional and personal life to figure out how I wanted to respond to feeling so thoroughly used up. As part of this process, Godbee passed on a piece of timeless advice: "If it's not a strong yes, it's a hell no."[27]

The suggestion to think about whether I was saying yes out of obligation, fear of missing out, some external measure of success, or genuine want was revolutionary to me. Whenever I thought of agreeing to something, I began asking myself if I was about to give a strong yes or a weak so-so answer that betrayed that in my heart of hearts I wasn't completely on board. There were times, of course, when people made requests of me that were demands in disguise, and moments where professionalism and/or care for others (especially junior faculty at my institution) meant I said yes to an obligation I might have turned down under different circumstances. But learning to ask if something is a strong yes has changed my relationship to saying no. It's not simply that I'm rejecting something; it's that I'm saying yes to something else, whether that's time, opportunity, or peace of mind.

I came across similar advice when I began following René Brooks on Twitter (@blkgirllostkeys). Brooks has ADHD and works as an advocate and coach for Black women with the same diagnosis. Among the educational work she does and the practical instruction she offers to others with ADHD, Brooks offers a key piece of advice: "Guard your yes with your life." Saying yes too often or too fast is, she argues, indicative of having too few boundaries and taking on too much responsibility for others. It can cause people to replicate dysfunctional patterns in their relationships and lead to overwork. Brooks's "Guard your yes" has become a watchword for me, and I have the phrase on a sticker stuck to the bottom of my computer screen.[28]

To these two pieces of wisdom I would add a third. Psychologist James Hollis suggests that, when facing decisions, we should ask ourselves, "Does this path, this choice, make me larger or smaller?"[29] This phrase is a game-changer, offering a way to think outside the unsteady framework of "What will make me happy?" There is every chance that if I say yes to a so-so request, for example, I may derive some happiness (or satisfaction, or career advancement) from completing the thing I've been asked to do. That still doesn't mean that it's the best use of my limited time or that it will offer me the meaningful engagement with the life (and work, and home, and community) that I long for. To ask if I am made smaller (jaded, compromised, put-upon) or larger (growing, savoring, challenging myself) helps me understand the quality of my yes.

Saying a strong yes may lead to conflict, just as saying no may; it is not an "ADVANCE TO GO (COLLECT $200)" card in the screwed-up game of academic Monopoly.[30] But by changing the parameters of the options I'm considering when I evaluate whether to take on a new responsibility, I've learned to reframe my answers as being the positive affirmation of myself rather than the rejection of others. It's hard to tell people no; it's hard—but so worthwhile—to learn to guard your yes.

8. Refuse to go it alone.

It is so thoroughly established that humans are social creatures as to make it hard to choose what to include in the footnote to this sentence: the evidence is almost dizzying in its abundance.[31] We depend so much upon our connections to others—socially, emotionally, and psychologically—that depriving people of human contact through solitary confinement is, for example, considered nothing less than torture under international law.[32] Many who had no prior experience of isolation experienced the early months of the COVID-19 pandemic as profoundly destabilizing; my own journal reminds me that, by May 2020, I was still committed to isolating myself to keep myself and others safe but felt unmoored, deeply touch-starved, and emotionally at sea.[33]

We function best when we are in community with others—although there is no singular form that such community should take. For some of us it's expressed through physical proximity to our colleagues, friends, and kin; for others it's about online socializing, networking, and support. The key thing is to recognize that community is deeply necessary to our well-being and identify the spaces and places where we might find, contribute to, and generate connection. For me this has taken a variety of forms: an in-person book group; hosting people for dinner at my home; a standing Friday-night cocktail hour over Zoom; texts and message boards; and diverse networks of friends and colleagues on Twitter. For others it might mean meeting with others who share a specific cultural background or faith tradition, working in a community garden, participating in a hiking group, or playing *Magic: The Gathering* with friends online. (These examples are all drawn from people I know.)

There's a tension between needing community and creating community: our lives do not always readily gift us the time and energy to create a community from scratch. And yet, finding community when we feel bereft of one is so important. Working in academia can be isolating, particularly if you're someone who's working multiple contingent jobs without a singular institutional home. Academia also often requires people to move, sometimes multiple times, across countries to secure a job. We are asked to begin again over and over—new cities, new institutions, new conditions of work. How do we make space for ourselves in relationship to others?

Writer Em Win offers a step-by-step guide to creating community in "How to Host a Restorative Dinner Party for Your Chosen Queer Fam." She suggests that the first step in creating a community setting is to "set your own intentions." As she elaborates, "Before you get to any planning or mingling, take some time to really think about what it is you want for this space. Sometimes it can be helpful to dream up a vision: who is there? where is it? what does it look like? how do you feel in the space? what are people saying about the space?"[34] I'd suggest that, whether or not you want to host a dinner party, setting intentions is a great way to approach the act of finding community. What is it that you hope to get from the experience? To contribute? Is there an absence in your life you're hoping to address? Equally, is there something present in your life that you want to amplify by engaging with others? Be clear-sighted about your motivations, hopes, and concerns.

Many of my communities are located online. In 2015, I joined Twitter because I had the sense that I was behind in adopting online tools to keep abreast of what was happening in my field. What I soon discovered was that on Twitter I had access to conversations that I could never have replicated offline. I teach at a small college where funding for travel to conferences, workshops, and research sites is limited. But on Twitter I could find my people for free: other individuals studying early America; librarians, archivists, and museum professionals; historians teaching at institutions similar to my own; and, crucially, a whole network of creative people invested in figuring out what constitutes good teaching. I could talk theory with professors at major research institutions and track down hard-to-find documents; I could find new ideas for teaching familiar subjects or tackling entirely new ones; I could help others decipher bad handwriting in a crucial document or post information about a lesson that really worked well. I started out by posting one thing a day—usually a retweet of something in the *Chronicle of Higher Education* or Inside Higher Ed (I wasn't very imaginative)—and I followed people I'd heard of and trusted, and then looked at who they followed to expand my feed. I began to interact with those people, and gradually people began to follow me back. Over time, my Twitter communities grew and not only became the primary way in which I interacted with others interested in history and teaching; they became the place where I discovered new ideas.

This is not to suggest that Twitter—like any social media—works for everyone or is devoid of hazards, particularly if you are a member of a marginalized community and particularly since recent changes in the ownership and management of Twitter/X itself. There are online trolls of every variety, for example, from the honestly misguided to the deeply malicious, and the time and attention they demand and the hatred they spew is emotionally, mentally, and sometimes even physically harmful.[35] But what worked for me with Twitter can work with Sprout, Mastodon, Post, Bluesky, or any other number of social media venues: do not be afraid to heavily curate your feed, to liberally use block features, and to mute conversations that are dragging on (in time) or dragging you down (in spirit). If online networking or socializing feels good to you, research the many platforms, apps, and message boards available. Read their terms of service; learn how they protect your privacy (or don't) and who's making money from the venture, so that you can make informed choices about the virtual spaces you want to occupy.[36]

If you'd prefer to seek community in person or to mix online and offline spaces, there are lots of ways to seek out new places to belong. In "Why Community Matters So Much—and How to Find Yours," Vox writer Allie Volpe suggests seeking out faith communities, volunteer organizations, or neighborhood groups, or googling a pastime that you've always wanted to invest in. Websites like Volunteer Match can connect you to a range of in-person volunteer opportunities in your area, as well connecting you to virtual ways to lend a hand. You can start small. As Jenny Anderson reports, "Community is about a series of small choices and everyday actions: how to spend a Saturday, what to do when a neighbor falls ill, how to make time when there is none. Knowing others and being known; investing in somewhere instead of trying to be everywhere. Communities are built, like Legos, one brick at a time.

There's no hack."[37] Join in where others have already done the work of organization. My campus has a tradition of individuals cooking food for people who've experienced a loss, undergone medical treatment, or added to their family, for example, and by participating I met people whose paths I might not otherwise have crossed.

When Self-Care Is Not the Answer

In April 2022, researchers Michelle A. Barton, Bill Kahn, Sally Maitlis, and Katherine M. Sutcliffe published "Stop Framing Wellness Programs around Self-Care" in the *Harvard Business Review*.[38] "As researchers who study employee well-being, resilience, and psychological health, we applaud the genuine concern" of organizations that asked workers to practice self-care, they wrote. "However, we are also increasingly concerned that the emphasis on self-care may undermine, rather than support, employee wellness."

The researchers' quarrel was not with the principle of people being cared for but rather with organizations and institutions placing the responsibility for wellness on individuals, which, they argued, led not toward much-needed community but toward disconnection. "When organizations offer individual solutions," wrote the researchers, "it can send the message that employees are on their own when it comes to their mental health." Instead of workers individually trying to wrangle any feelings of distress they might be experiencing, the researchers suggested that people should be encouraged to view adversity as a collective problem. "Rather than focusing on *self-care*, we need to be better at *taking care of each other*," they wrote. The researchers were not suggesting that organizations outsource care work to people with the least institutional power. Instead, they asserted that organizational leaders must create an environment in which it was clear that an individual's struggle was shared.

Barton and colleagues suggested that leaders create moments of "relational pause" where people could talk about the situations, events, and feelings shaping their work life. "Importantly, the goal is not psychoanalysis or personal therapy, and it is not a 'pity party' or 'whining,'" they clarified. "The process does not even require people to be friends. Rather, it is discussion with a purpose: to surface and acknowledge the emotional reality of work that might otherwise be ignored, and to actively help group members engage productively with that reality." Allowing room to tell the truth, they argued, would create resilient connection and community.

The work of these researchers suggests something that most of us know: we cannot leave our emotions at the door when we show up (online or off) to do our jobs. As psychologist Sarah Rose Cavanagh explains, there is no neat and tidy divide between intellectual work and how we're feeling: "Emotion is already present in all experience, perhaps even particularly so in cognition," she writes. Neuroscientist Mary Helen Immordino-Yang concurs arguing that "it is literally neurobiologically impossible to build memories, engage complex thoughts, or make mean-ingful decisions without emotion."[39] When we experience loss, depres-sion, and anxiety; when we have triumphs to celebrate; when we are harassed and discriminated against; when we feel joy—those feelings live inside us and move with us into the academic spaces we occupy. Whether we can give expression to those feelings as Barton and colleagues sug-gest, however, is deeply tied to considerations of gender, sexuality, and race. The intellectual ideal in pop culture, in the social imagination, and in the very real terms of who has power at our institutions is a dispas-sionate, older white man who is happy to live a life of the mind, pretend-ing that emotions are of little consequence.[40] There have long been risks inherent in anyone else vocalizing their feelings—charges that we are hysterical or too angry—even before a global pandemic brought greater pressure to bear upon our lives.[41]

The task of establishing a collective ethos of care is inseparable from tackling the injustices alive and well on our campuses. If we are to pause in relation to one another—adjunct and president, student and member of the governing board—to communicate and take care of one another, we need a foundation of genuine respect. Without it, collective care is merely a performance, a product of prioritizing niceness while funda-mentally avoiding the responsibility of being kind.

Some institutions are responding. The Ohio State University, for example, has made a wealth of self-care resources available to its fac-ulty and staff.[42] Crucially, however, it has also updated its personnel policies to offer practical and financial support to some of its employ-ees in the form of $125-per-quarter wellness reimbursements to those who are "full-time and part-time (at least 50% FTE) in a regular or term position." These funds can be used for sports fees or dance classes but also for arts and crafts supplies, board games, memberships to the zoo, or financial counseling (among many other options).[43] The institution has also introduced "Back-Up Care" to cover unexpected childcare or in-home care needs, and subsidizes the cost.[44] While these programs should be expanded to cover everyone who works for the university, and to not rely on individuals fronting the costs, these are positive steps. Similarly, the University of Notre Dame offers a "Compassion Fund" to eligible faculty and staff to help cover the costs related to fire, theft, illness, or other unexpected expenses, although there are limits on who can receive help and how often. Notre Dame's graduate college offers an emergency fund for natural disasters, a damaged computer, or temporary housing.[45] These are helpful models for administrators to consider.

But what do we do now, in the time between now and the realization of change from the top down? One approach is to modify Barton and colleagues' vision and share material, social, and emotional burdens among our coworkers and friends. Karen Costa has been considering these questions for some time. "The system works to protect those in power," she writes. "It doesn't care about what's right or kind or effective or logical. So, facing that reality feels increasingly important to me, and I think mutual aid is one of the things I've found that actually operates within that reality."[46] Dean Spade offers a good definition of mutual aid: "Collective coordination to meet each other's needs, usually from an awareness that the systems we have in place are not going to meet them. Those systems, in fact, have often created the crisis or made things worse."[47] As Representative Alexandria Ocasio-Cortez and organizer Mariame Kaba add, "It means we recognize that our well-being, health and dignity are all bound up in each other. It means that we understand our survival depends on cooperation, not competition."[48] Costa sees mutual aid happening all around us—in actions to lobby for, protect, and create the circumstances for reproductive justice to flourish; in the communities of care that sprang up around emergency lifeboat learning in the early period of the pandemic; in networks of educators who are refusing to engage in what Costa calls "toxic rigor." "It's in the small connections and communities. It's already here and we're already doing it. Now the work is to amplify it and watch it grow," Costa writes.[49]

To come together to create a mutual aid network, we should not only identify a need within our communities, but also the reason the need exists. This is a necessarily political act, one that critiques the structures within which such a need is created and/or embedded. Mutual aid then mobilizes people to respond to that need and by avoiding hierarchical organization (or looking for single saviors to figure things out) builds solidarity between everyone involved.[50] Mutual aid organizations already exist on many of our campuses and have for a while; students have created and sustained them to step in where universities are unable or unwilling to address particular situations. Students have provided each other with money for housing, food, and books, created food pantries, and established emergency housing entirely outside their institutions' formal structures.[51] These are material needs that many faculty and staff also need help in meeting, especially where campuses are located in high cost-of-living areas, where individuals are burdened by student loans, where new workers have to wait four to eight weeks for their first paycheck, and where employees have extended kinship responsibilities.

We can also stretch the meaning of mutual aid and ask what pedagogical mutual aid might look like. Take something as simple as office supplies, the cost of which quickly adds up if you're someone who—because of your junior or contingent status—has to cover them yourself, or if you work for a college where even the paper clip budget has been cut. If you have access to a budget line, make sure at least some of it is used to provide pens, pencils, Post-its, notepads, printer paper, staplers, staples, whiteboard markers, chalk, and, yes, paperclips for grad students, contingent faculty, and part-time workers. If budget lines are empty or you're left to fend for yourself, consider establishing a central fund for office supplies or a hub where you and others in a similar boat can pool what you have—where anyone can pick up basic necessities and where there are perhaps sets of markers or colored pencils or poster-sized sticky notes that can be borrowed, used in class, and returned. (I have a whole range of construction tools in my office, for example, thanks to years of teaching a museum class where my students create exhibits. Not everyone needs a steady supply of painter's tape, hammers, tacks, or three-foot rulers, but everyone in my department knows where to find those things when circumstances demand it.) Office supplies may seem a small thing, but they are not insignificant. I vividly remember when I was living on a graduate student stipend and had to sneak into the history office to pilfer some index cards to use in class because I could not afford to provide them myself. People need the tools to do their work effectively and creatively. Where's the need where you work, and how can you collaboratively meet it?

A pedagogical mutual aid group might take many other forms. Consider creating a collection of syllabi and sample assignments to which everyone can contribute and that everyone can browse. Perhaps the collection is in a filing cabinet on-site; perhaps it's in Google Drive; ideally both exist to maximize access. Such an archive can draw from the wisdom of people who have been teaching creatively for a long time, but also from the fresh ideas and energy of brand-new educators. Within departments, such a collection can also encourage the breaking down of hierarchies and an investment in everyone's expertise. And the sharing of documents can be done between any mutually interested group of people anywhere. Where a single department on a single campus does not represent your teaching "home,'" use chat boards and social media to find colleagues who can support you and whom you can support. Similarly, consider how digital know-how can be pooled within your group, with different people sharing their expertise in the use of varied software, platforms, or campus learning management systems. If you're someone who could make good use of this sort of expertise but don't have digital know-how to share in return, think about what might you offer to ensure the mutuality of this kind of exchange. We all have skills and insights that others can learn from, no matter our rank, years in service, or status as faculty or staff.

When we think about pedagogy, we most often think about students—about how to reach them, inspire them, work with them, and facilitate their growth. But pedagogy can't exist without teachers and—in a phrase that's often repeated by those with an interest in education—student learning conditions are teacher working conditions. If we want to make kindness a guiding principle of our pedagogy—to thread it through our syllabi, assignments, class activities, and the homework we assign—we have to begin by being kind to ourselves. This is not about doing yoga, listening to a great piece of music, or sitting outside for five minutes and listening to birdsong (although those are all wonderful things to do). It's about making a promise to ourselves that we are worthy of care and that our colleagues are as well. It's about committing ourselves to the work of justice on our campuses in every place we touch. It's about reconciliation, forgiveness, and accountability. It's about saying yes and owning our no to create the conditions under which we can be the teachers we and our students deserve. It's about extending support to one another and dismantling isolation. It's about making kindness the bedrock of all we do.

2

KINDNESS AND THE SYLLABUS

The first day of a course often revolves around a syllabus, and our work to embed kindness in our teaching should begin in the same place. To frame our course syllabi as instruments of kindness may require us to rethink our usual relationship to those carefully crafted documents. When I wrote my first syllabus, I replicated all the syllabi I'd seen up until that point in my life. My syllabus was filled with walls of text—a document that, from the very outset, looked intimidating. In it, I tried to anticipate where things could go wrong over the duration of a semester, articulated rules in response to that fear, and outlined the penalties that would follow if someone messed up. I had lists of assignment dates and the readings I wanted my students to do, but nothing that told them how to approach that reading or the sorts of questions with which I hoped they would wrestle. I also included the things I was required to put into a syllabus: boilerplate language about disability services and the rules surrounding sexual harassment, for example. During graduate school you wouldn't have been able to differentiate my syllabus from those handed to me by my undergraduate professors, whose example I wanted to avoid in most things. But it never occurred to me to question a syllabus's form. As far as I could tell, dense, textual, legalistic syllabi were the way that business was done.

There's something comforting, perhaps, about the idea that the syllabus is a legalistic contract articulating the responsibilities of the instructor (office hours, email address, presence in some kind of classroom on certain days and times) and of students (coming to class, doing the reading, solving the problem sets, turning in the assignments). We try to make the contract clear, fiddling with our syllabi to anticipate every question a student could have about a course. Some of us have experienced real conflict around the form and content of our syllabi, whether that conflict has been with members of an administration, colleagues, or students themselves, so we're sometimes playing defense before it can happen again. After all of this, we therefore despair if students then pose questions we know we've already answered in our syllabus; we're sometimes irritated when we have to explain concepts, policies, or assignments again. Small wonder, then, that constructing a syllabus can feel to many of us like a chore, unrelated to the best parts of teaching.

The fact is that very few of us are trained in how to build a good syllabus, and that has consequences: many of us end up replicating the banking model of education that Paulo Freire critiqued more than fifty years ago. Too many models of education, he argued, saw instructors create narratives about the subject matter of their courses that students were meant to passively absorb. "Education thus becomes an act of depositing, in which the students are the depositories, and the teacher is the depositor. Instead of communicating, the teacher issues communiqués and makes deposits which the students patiently receive, memorize, and repeat," he wrote. "In the banking concept of education, knowledge is a gift bestowed by those who consider themselves knowledgeable upon those whom they consider to know nothing."[1] Freire's critique is especially apt when we think about syllabi. We often conceive of the syllabus as a description of the things we want students to passively receive.

But we can change that. I first grasped that there were other ways to approach a syllabus at the Digital Pedagogy Lab Institute in 2017, where Chris Friend and Sean Michael Morris, the facilitators of the Intro track, asked us question after question about our intentions and goals for—and the authorial voice we used in—our syllabi. I realized that the syllabus was one of the very first entry points for students to get to know me; the document was (and is) relational. The legalistic tone I took in my syllabus suggested I was remote, authoritarian, and inherently suspicious of my students, and I realized that no matter how I showed up in our physical classroom, my syllabus was creating a first impression antithetical to who I hoped to be. I could exert some degree of control over that by making conscious choices about language use and design by creating a syllabus that reflected my actual values and priorities and by asking students to interact with the syllabus in meaningful ways. While no syllabus sets the tone for a course in utter isolation, I could rethink my syllabus to do the greatest share of relational work that it could.

Make no mistake: the work is deeply relational. No syllabus acts as a pure download of information from instructor to student. As Donna

Mejia articulates, "Students arrive at our learning space with their own baggage and habituated relationships with authority figures."[2] Students compare our syllabi to other syllabi they've read; they reflect on whether they've read those boilerplate statements before; they decide what looks like filler and what looks important. Crucially, students decide how much of the syllabus they should invest time in reading based on whether they've navigated other courses and, if so, how they did it. When students choose not to read the syllabus in the way we wish, it's rarely because of laziness or hubris; instead it's a reflection of their experience (or lack of it) in parsing courses for themselves. The ingrained habit of many instructors to go over the syllabus on the first day of class suggests that we'll tell them what's important and they can probably gloss over the rest. Students also assess the syllabus in relation to how we look, how we speak, and whether we seem comfortable in our virtual or physical classroom. They then compare that information—consciously or unconsciously—with their beliefs about who is the "right" kind of instructor, a "rightness" that is stitched together from past experiences, prejudices, and sometimes hope.[3]

To understand the syllabus as a relational document, then, is to understand it to be a complex overture to learning. We must give serious thought to the invitations we offer through the document, to the boundaries we articulate, and to the spaces we leave open for collaboration. This means there is no easy how-to for a syllabus that works for your particular circumstances. Beyond the schedule of topics, readings, lab sections, and viewings, which pretty much everyone agrees are important syllabus content, there is little agreement "out there" as to the perfect length of a syllabus or what it should include.[4] Yet, if we are serious about our syllabi acting as useful sources of information for our students we need to, once again, think carefully about who our students are and what they need to succeed. I can't tell you if your syllabus should be three pages or fifteen, nor can I supply exactly the right language for your situation. I can, however, suggest that we think deeply about what we and our students might need from a document that offers structure to a course.

Who Is the Student You're Imagining As You Write?

If you'd asked me who I thought I was as a teacher in the spring of 2017, I would have said that I was someone who valued community, one-on-one student relationships, and the collective discovery of ideas. I would probably have explained that I rarely lectured, as I didn't think it produced the kind of learning in which I wanted my students to partic-ipate, and that even when I did lecture it was for no longer than fifteen to twenty minutes. I might have talked about the fact that my office door was always open—physically and metaphorically—to my students. I felt pretty good about my pedagogical self.

But that summer at the Digital Pedagogy Lab, Chris Friend and Sean Michael Morris asked everyone in the Intro track whether our syllabi actually communicated collaboration, inclusion, transparency, and the kind of relationship we wanted to build with our students. I had to con-fess that mine didn't—in fact, my course documents communicated that I was distant and unfeeling and, worse, that students were constantly in danger of screwing up and losing my favor. This came as an actual physical shock.

In early 2017, my syllabi cold-opened with my contact information in a format that was not particularly welcoming or easy to parse:

Professor: Cate Denial
Office: [building and room number]
Office Phone: [number and extension]
Office Hours: Tuesday and Wednesday, 11am-noon
Email: cdenial@knox.edu (9am to 9pm, except 5pm Friday to
        5pm Sat.)

Compare this to the beginning of my more recent syllabi, captured in the illustration on the following page.

The shifts in language and design between these two examples may seem small, but they added up to a big difference in what and how I com-municated to my students. Even small shifts in tone have a big impact on student perceptions of their instructor's willingness to help them.[5] I opened with a greeting where I had dispensed with such courtesies in my original syllabus. I welcomed the students; I included my pronouns not only for clarity's sake but to communicate that I welcomed students of every gender (and no gender at all). I then segued into information about how students could reach me, but I did so with full sentences, and I was transparent about why I limited my time on email. (I increased the amount of time I took away from email as a kindness to myself.) I also placed an icon on the left of the page so that students skimming the document later in the term would quickly be able to find the details for which they were looking.

You might want to go further and include an even more in-depth wel-come in your syllabus by sharing biographical information or language

Hi, I'm Cate Denial, and I'll be your professor this term. Welcome to the class! My pronouns are she/her/hers.

You can reach me by email at cdenial@knox.edu

I'm available by email from 9am-8pm M-Th and 9am to 4pm on Friday.

Saturdays and Sundays are my recharge days, so I will occasionally check my email, but cannot guarantee you a quick reply on those days.

Student Hours:

My student hours are from noon to 1pm on Mondays, Wednesdays, and Fridays, and I am delighted to meet with you over Zoom at other times. Just email me to make an appointment!

The beginning of my syllabus.

that explains why you're excited to teach a particular course. As Kevin Gannon suggests in his advice about building syllabi in the *Chronicle of Higher Education,* "If you drew the short straw in the departmental rotation and are teaching [a course] because no one else wanted to, perhaps it's best not to say so. But usually there is something about the course—it's in your area of specialization, it's one of your personal favorites, you enjoy introducing nonmajors to your discipline—that drew you to it. Tell your students what that is, and invite them to share that interest with you."[6] You can also include—in written, audio, or video form—a little of your teaching philosophy. I direct my students to my teaching website, where they can find a video I made explaining who I am and how I approach instruction.[7] Michelle Pacansky-Brock suggests that if we take inclusion and belonging seriously, we should go further, as "students who identify with one or more non-dominant identity groups—which include, but are not restricted to, students who are Black, Latina/o/x, Indigenous and other people of color; physically or cognitively different; members of the LGBTIQA+ community; low-income; older; non-native English speakers—are more likely to have experienced oppression and discrimination in their previous educational experiences and are more likely to enter a college course from a place of distrust." Pacansky-Brock suggests providing students with a welcome video a week before classes begin, the timing and medium offering "verbal and nonverbal cues, which are [the] safety cues a human brain scans for in a state of threat," thereby defusing the tension that students might feel.[8] All of these approaches seek to demystify who we are as instructors, turning us from formless, generic educators into people, and establishing how we wish to be known.

Elsewhere in my syllabus, my language choices underwent a profound overhaul. Here's what my syllabi said about my college's honor code in spring 2017:

> The Knox College community expects its members to demonstrate a high degree of ethical integrity in all their actions, including their academic work. Examples of academic dishonesty include plagiarism, giving or receiving unauthorized help, voluntarily assisting another student in cheating, and dishonestly obtaining an extension. If you have any questions about this, or if you are panicking about your ability to meet deadlines, please come and talk with me.
>
> Please re-acquaint yourself with the Knox College Honor Code at [URL].*

My words said nothing about trust and therefore implied that all my students stood at the precipice of committing terrible offenses. I did not define the words I used. A first-year student might not know what plagiarism was; neither might a student from a wholly different discipline, unfamiliar with the conventions of practicing history. What exactly did I have in mind when I said students shouldn't give or receive "unauthorized help"? It wasn't clear. Nevertheless, I had once felt proud of this language, especially because I acknowledged that panic was often at work when a student faltered in their attempt to do the right thing.[9]

I replaced this language immediately. From fall 2017 onward, the same section of my syllabus read:

> We commit ourselves to act with academic integrity this term—to be ethical in what we say and write, and to offer credit to others for thinking of ideas before us. I believe that everyone in my course is

---

* The Knox College honor code for the 2016–17 and 2017–18 academic years is no longer online. As of this writing, the 2022–23 honor code may be seen at https://www.knox.edu/documents/AcademicAffairs/Honor_System.pdf.

fundamentally honest, and I will help you learn the conventions of academic integrity, such as citing sources correctly and being clear about where our own words begin and end.

    If you'd like to read more about the college's Honor Code—which was written by students just like you, and which students co-govern with faculty—you can find a copy at this link: [URL].

Here, I offered a plain-language definition of academic integrity as well as a concrete example of what that looked like in my discipline. I also said, very clearly, that I believed my students were honest, a change that accurately reflected my beliefs about them and that served to emphasize that I was entering into a general relationship with them based upon trust. I also took responsibility for teaching students how to act with academic integrity, something my previous statement had omitted altogether.

    I also changed the way I thought about attendance. The following is my attendance policy from 2016—a mash-up of my own language and language borrowed from a syllabus provided as a model by another institution:

> The outcome of this course relies on your informed, honest, and active involvement. You are allowed two unexcused absences during the course, but your attendance is expected at all other times. Excused absences include serious illness or family emergency, and cultural and religious holidays with notification. Though I hope no one experiences an illness or family emergency, if you do, please inform me as soon as possible—ideally, in advance of the class meeting. Make-up work may be assigned. If you have a religious or cultural holiday that conflicts with a class meeting or activity, notify me by Monday, March 27 so I can make sure that you have an excused absence for this day. If I do not hear from you by Monday, March 27 I will assume that you plan to attend all class sessions, and full attendance will be required.

    Whether to require attendance in a course is a subject on which there is wide debate, and there are often circumstances where an instructor might set a strict attendance policy as one part of helping students learn how to prioritize time and energy.[10] But my language choices communicated distrust. They reflected my underlying sense that students sometimes entered my class without a proper commitment to learning and would miss class for "no good reason" if given the chance. This was a terrible way to begin a relationship with students. I went back to the drawing board, revising my language (which all of us can do) and revisiting my attachment to an attendance policy in the first place (which may or may not be the policy you personally want to adopt). I wanted my language to reflect that I saw students as collaborators in their learning; I wanted to acknowledge their complicated lives and not add to these complications; I wanted to speak with compassion. My new policy, developed in conversation with friends and colleagues, looked like this:

> As co-collaborators in creating our learning space this term, we'll be relying on each other's informed, honest, and active involvement in class discussions.
>
> I realize different people participate in conversation in different ways, and that for some students, speaking in public is difficult. If you have any concerns about this, come and see me so that together we can work out the best way for you to participate in the class.
>
> It's important for us all to remember that different communities possess different culturally specific norms about how to best engage in a conversation, and for us to make room for this expression.
>
> Remember to listen to one another, and to support your colleagues in their discovery of new ideas, their questions, and their articulation of thought. We'll crowdsource a list of conversational guidelines during the first week of classes.
>
> If you have to miss any of our classes know that we will miss your presence. Please email me to let me know you'll be absent so that I can support you and help you catch up afterwards.

I went through every part of my syllabus in this way. I identified all the places where I'd said "I will" or "you will" and replaced them with "we will" as appropriate. I asked myself why I had phrased things as I had and if there wasn't a better way to do so—a way that was rooted in kindness. I thought long and hard about who my students were and what they needed from me in order to succeed. In every instance I realized that a preemptive scolding through the syllabus on the first day of class was not how I wanted to begin.

Does Your Syllabus Tackle Issues of Justice?

In education, we are all engaged in (or disengaged from) the production of knowledge. The syllabus is where this begins, cuing our students to anticipate the kind of knowledge we believe in and with which we want to wrestle. Just as we cannot be good teachers while living unexamined lives, we cannot be good teachers while writing unexamined syllabi. The academy is built upon a long, violent history of exclusion. The life of the mind (and body) offered by colleges and universities has, for the majority of its existence, privileged the experiences, thoughts, and feelings of wealthy white men and, without our critical intervention, will continue to do so.[11]

This means we must ask ourselves a series of important questions. Who are represented in our syllabi and who are not? Are the writers, artists, scholars, and scientists to whom we direct our students' attention a racially and ethnically diverse group of thinkers and creators? Do they come from varied class backgrounds, hold different gender identities, and include people with disabilities? Where are they located in the world? What relationship do they have to citizenship in the place(s) they live? Will our students see themselves reflected back from the curriculum, or will they be implicitly told they come from cultures and traditions without knowledge the academy deems worthy of respect? We must bring this analysis to bear on our syllabi as we craft the intellectual spaces our students will enter.

Even after asking and answering these questions, there may occasions when, for example, the best textbooks in your field, for a whole variety of reasons, are written by those whom society has rewarded with an inequitable share of social and political power. It is our job as educators to then contextualize that situation for our students and to ask who has been invited to contribute to the stores of knowledge we examine, why, by whom, and under what circumstances. The students we teach come from an ever-expanding number of communities, and if we invite them to the seminar table or lab space, they should find intellectual nourishment of every kind. We begin every semester with a syllabus. Who will find belonging in that document and who will be turned away?

Justice is central to the work of constructing a syllabus—and not just in terms of the knowledge it offers. Our students' academic performance is conditioned by a great deal more than their aptitude, their ambition, or their talent. It depends on having access to a steady supply of nutritious food, a safe place of shelter, access to technology and an internet connection, a learning environment in which their humanity is not questioned, and an environment that anticipates—rather than just accommodates— disabilities.[12] There are offices, divisions, and departments on all our campuses to help us in supporting students in all of these situations. But students have to know those places exist to take them up on their services. This means our syllabi should contain a range of important information:

- Resources for students who are hungry or lack shelter. (On the Knox campus that means directing people to the Division of Student Development, which has a short-term, interest-free loan program, a food pantry, and vast experience dealing with problems related to housing.)
- Resources for students who lack a computer or internet connection. (This means directing students to public computer labs—a map will help students navigate a large campus—to resources like laptop rentals from your library or information technology department, and to other reliable sources of free internet, like a public library.)
- Resources for students—beyond the first-line help you can provide—who are struggling with planning, organization, content comprehension, research, writing, and understanding a professor's feedback. (On the Knox campus this means directing them to writing tutors and subject tutors and knowing the hours and locations where such help is available. It also means directing them to the library and the librarian connected to our course.)
- Resources for students who have experienced discrimination, harassment, and assault based on any protected category. (This means you know where to find your institution's policies on these matters and can offer students contact information for the heads of diversity, equity, inclusion, and belonging on your campus as well as whoever is responsible for responding to Title IX complaints. If your campus has identified you, your TA, your resident assistant, or another individual as a responsible or mandated reporter for Title IX, put this information in your syllabus so that students can make informed choices about to whom they would like to speak.)
- Resources for students experiencing physical and/or mental health challenges. (Provide every means of reaching these services that your campus has: email, web address, phone number, chat line, software app. Different students will need different means of reaching out for help according to their personal preferences and variables like the time of day.)
- Resources for students with disabilities. Many institutions provide boilerplate language about accommodations for student disabilities to ensure that all instructors comply with the law. Almost all institutions have an office of disability services that

coordinates accommodation requests, assesses the documentation a student supplies about their disability, and offers a
first point of contact for a student whose professors refuse to
follow accommodation rules. This, I would suggest, is the bare
minimum that should be in your syllabus. Not all students
can afford the testing or medical visits that are necessary to
document a disability to the satisfaction of a disability services
office. This means educating ourselves about some broad categories of flexibility that can be worked into assignment and
class activity design and telling students we're ready to help.
(More on this in chapter three).

How Have You Planned Your (and Your Students') Time?

As educators, we know an enormous amount about our fields, and we
tend to think that most of what we know is vitally important. We want to
pass that knowledge along to our students, and so, springing from our
enthusiasm for the subject and with the very best of intentions, we often
cram content into our courses like sardines into a can. I teach history.
There's a painfully accurate joke about historians that says that if you ask
us to explain an event that happened last week, we'll start the explanation with something that happened four centuries before.[13] I have lived
up to this stereotype in multiple ways and, as an early-career scholar,
spent hours deliberating over exactly how much I could ask students
to engage with in a given term. If someone had asked me about my
course goals as a first-year professor in 2005, I would have said "to teach
students as much about this subject as I possibly can." Only once I had
packed the schedule with readings and documentaries did I slot in all
the graded assignments—and did so assuming that students would be
able to fulfill the terms of those assignments without breaking a sweat.

I had it all backward. What I learned over time was that I needed a
clearer sense of where I hoped students would end up by the end of the
course and that if I wanted them to get there I had to create learning
opportunities that would encourage them to reach that goal. Learning
goals, as they're known in most of academia, are sometimes fraught
concepts connected to the assessment demands of our institutions
and the accreditation agencies that look at the books once every ten
years.[14] Under certain circumstances they can feel artificial and forced
or overly prescriptive, preventing students from discovering and delin-
eating their own agendas for their learning.[15] Still, I've come to think of

learning goals as a helpful map that can guide students—who can absolutely decide the route—to a particular destination. They provide structure to students who need it and are easily accompanied by an exercise in which I ask students to write their own goals for their learning in any given term. At their best, learning goals help my students and me to keep our eyes on the horizon and chart the long-term trajectory of what we hope to achieve.

When I began to reflect on the direction my courses might take, I realized skills were at least as important, if not more important, than content. If a student learned the right skills, they'd be able to track down the answers to their questions for the rest of their lives. If I only taught content, they would likely forget a great deal of detail and have no good idea how to find trustworthy sources in the future. That felt deeply antithetical to the point of a history education—just as it would be antithetical to the vast majority of what we do no matter our field. I therefore made a list of the skills I thought would serve my students in their hopefully very long lives, and the content I thought it was important that they know, and then asked myself: If I want to end up *there*, what do we have to do *here*? Working backward from the end of the course, I asked myself five questions over and over again:

- If I want students to be able to do (x goal) by (x date), when do I need to starting teaching them the skills and content they'll need to succeed in that?
- How will I know if the students have succeeded? What assessments should I include and how should they be paced?
- How much time do I need to fully participate in the assessment process? How does that effect the timing of assignments? (Overestimate the time it will take for you to provide feedback or grade your students' work. In my first years as an educator, I did not schedule any time to grade at all, which left me hopelessly overwhelmed when it came to grading 120 midterm exams in my first year as a teaching assistant.)
- Where can I build in space and time so that we can embrace the unexpected, or pursue threads my students really want to follow, or give everyone a mental health break?
- And finally: What should my students read, watch, or hear in order to make all of this possible?[16]

Building a syllabus this way involves a lot of trial and error—a lot of penciling things in and erasing them, a lot of Post-it Notes moved around, a lot of ideas recorded on an electronic calendar that get deleted or cut and pasted and resituated again. But designing a class schedule this way helps us to avoid the common pitfall of trying to cram sardines of knowledge into our students' brains and allows serendipity to have a place in the classroom spaces we co-create. Assume that you will need to teach your students how to succeed in your class. If you want them to read, teach them the conventions of how books and articles in your field are organized and why. If you want them to follow your directions in the lab, explain to them why specific protocols exist. If you want them to conduct interviews, facilitate a conversation about the ethics and responsibilities inherent in doing so. And do not schedule every minute of every single day. Allow space for unexpected moments to occur.

All of this extends to the ritual of understanding a syllabus too. A syllabus is such a familiar document to instructors that we often forget what it was like to learn to read one for the first time. There are lots of ways a syllabus might be a first in the lives of our students: we teach first-year students of all ages; we teach students entering the first course in their major; we work with students returning after a break from school. If we presume that the form of our syllabus is familiar to students, we stand to lose some of our students' engagement from the get-go—not because they are uninterested in our course content, but because they feel lost. We need to write in such a way as to be clearly understood, and we need to teach our students to interact with syllabi as texts without making assumptions about their ability to do so without guidance. Just as we teach our students how to read books, articles, data sets, and works of art, teaching others how to read the documents that provide structure to a course is no different. A syllabus that is created with compassion is an exercise in language, design (or appearance), accessibility, and clarity, and can make room for collaboration.

If our syllabi are to provide meaningful structure to the courses we teach, they have to reach every student in the class. Walls of text don't do this: they can appear dense and off-putting to even the most savvy of students, and for students who find reading and organizing information a real challenge, they place an obstacle in the path of their learning from day one. Imagine the most jargon-filled, theoretically dense, and complicated piece of reading you've ever done in your academic life, and the physical and mental struggle to absorb the information it contained. Now imagine being given that text on day one of your undergraduate education. That's often what a syllabus represents to our students, especially when they are novices at interacting with the genre.

HIST 167, Fall 2020

The History of Gender and Sexuality in the U.S.

Hi, I'm Cate Denial, and I'll be your professor this term. Welcome to the class! My pronouns are she/her/hers.

How to reach me:

Email: cdenial@knox.edu

I'm available by email from 9am-8pm M-Th and 9am to 4pm Friday.

Saturdays and Sundays are my recharge days, so I will occasionally check my email, but cannot guarantee you a quick reply on those days.

Student Hours:

My student hours are from 9-10.30am on Wednesdays and Fridays, and I am delighted to meet with you over Zoom at other times. Just email me to make an appointment!

A plaintext version of my syllabus.

One key to writing an accessible syllabus is to break up the text and offer clear directions to students about where to find the information they need. This may mean a largely textual syllabus with lots of white space, precise subheadings, and short paragraphs of information. It may mean taking steps to create syllabi that contain lots of visual cues, such as colorful headers and icons that direct students to policies and to support service information.[17] No one needs to be a graphic designer or possess innate artistic talent to create such a document, thanks to websites such as Canva and Venngage (templates and visual organizers), Pexels and Freepik (free photography), and Flaticon and Storyset (icons and illustrations).[18] The header in the syllabus below was made by my colleague Yvonne Seale using illustrations from Canva, while I took a screenshot of a Google mail icon from my account.

As you design, keep accessibility in mind. Choose a font that is easy for students to read. I remember being taught in graduate school that serif fonts could blur on a student's computer screen and make each letter

HIST 167, Fall 2020
The History of Gender and Sexuality in the U.S.

Hi, I'm Cate Denial, and I'll be your professor this term. Welcome to the class!
My pronouns are she/her/hers.

You can reach me in the following ways:

Email: cdenial@knox.edu

I'm available by email from 9am-8pm M-Th and 9am to
4pm Friday.

Saturdays and Sundays are my recharge days, so I will
occasionally check my email, but cannot guarantee you a
quick reply on those days.

An image-based syllabus. Header image by Yvonne Seale.

hard to discern, so I favored sans serif fonts for most of my academic career. Until quite recently, I did not know that advances in computer technology—including better lit, clearer screen displays—meant that this was not as much a concern as it had been in the 1990s. It's still worth thinking about those fonts that have been designed with accessibility in mind, such as Open Sans, Lexie Readable, or Atkinson Hyperlegible, while understanding there is no single font that will speak to every student's need.[19] There are other choices that also maximize the accessibility of syllabus design. Avoid using a lot of green and red on your syllabus in case you have students who have color vision deficiency, which is a common occurrence, especially among men.[20] When using headers or icons, make sure you embed alternative text within those images for students who use screen readers to access course documents. This is a simple process within Word or Google Docs: right click on an image for a menu that includes the alt text choice on a PC, and on a Mac press CTRL and click your mouse on the image itself. Avoid the use of tables, which are hard for screen readers to parse. Use boldfaced text sparingly so that it

offers a meaningful cue to students when it is used, and try to avoid italics, which often suggest negative emphasis.[21] When your syllabus is complete, listen to your design using read-aloud software that will alert you to
places where your document is inaccessible. Ann Gagné offers more suggestions on creating accessible documents in her podcast, *Accessagogy*.[22]

What if We Let Students Build the Syllabus Themselves?

One of the most creative ways to build a document your students will
value is to have them write the syllabus for themselves. What do they
think it's important to include? What do they have to say about the shape
of assessment and the frequency of assignments? What policies do they
value? Students look at many more syllabi in their lives that we do,
from all kinds of disciplines, and have a strong sense of when a syllabus
has worked for them and when it has not. Having students draft their
own syllabi, and then facilitating a larger conversation about the things
included and left out, turns the syllabus into a metacognitive project.[23]
There will, of course, be conflicts between certain people's expectations,
but that's when discussion is particularly important to build consensus
among the class members.

On the first day of my history pedagogy class in 2019, I distributed
a syllabus that had the name of the course on it, a header image, and
then three blank sheets of paper. My students' homework was to come
up with a syllabus that they thought should provide structure to the
course. During the next class period, I put students into small groups
and gave them large, poster-sized sticky notes on which to draft a syllabus that drew on the best ideas they'd collectively dreamed up. I then
asked them the same question Chris Friend and Sean Michael Morris
had once asked me: Who was the student they explicitly or implicitly
had had in mind when they wrote this document? Every group walked
around the room, read every other group's syllabus, and left thoughts
on small Post-it Notes about how they felt as a student reading the policies and expectations their classmates had expressed. I recently asked
some of the former students from that class to reflect on that exercise
and what they learned. "This assignment confronted my entire belief
system on how professors communicate with students and the expectations that I had based on the standard that other teachers/professors
had set," said Courtney Pletcher. "The language/diction that is used in
syllabi can set the tone between the professor and student before the
professor has formally introduced themselves to a student."[24] Kylie

Hoang agreed: the exercise, "illuminated something deeper with other instructors/the higher ed system as a whole. . . . I realized how little other instructors trusted me."[25] After the class, "when professors used a cookie cutter syllabus and placed emphasis on heavy grading and the Honor Code . . . those were the professors who were usually unaccommodating to personal situations or unwilling to help students when they needed additional assistance/tutoring," added Courtney. There were more immediate effects too. "We treated the syllabus as a collaborative document and any changes made after the semester [began] were made as a group. At the very least that made me feel more invested in reading and understanding the whole document," said Kylie.

This is a scalable exercise. In larger classes, consider having students work in small groups to devise a syllabus and then swap their prototype with one or two other groups to get feedback. After the opportunity for analysis and conversation, give students the chance to distill down the conclusions they've drawn from the exercise and offer a verbal or written report about what they think it's most important to include in the syllabus, how, and why. Be willing to make changes to your syllabus document in response. You'll end up with a collectively sourced syllabus in which students have a greater investment, and you'll have had a little fun in making syllabus construction a transparent act.

You Have a Syllabus—Now What?

After spending a great deal of time thinking about your syllabus comes the next question: How do you get your students to engage with the document in a meaningful way and remember that it contains information that is vital to their experience in your class?

For the greater portion of my teaching career, I followed the tried-and-tested ritual of going over the syllabus in class on the first day of the semester. This was, I'll be frank, a stultifying introduction to my courses. I was bored and I can only imagine my students were too; the highlight of such class periods was letting everyone leave early. I had no idea if students had absorbed any of the information on the syllabus or not but definitely assumed they'd read it later. It took me some time to realize I was cuing them to do anything but. Why would they assume that I would omit important information from my highlight reel in class?

But then I read Remi Kalir's excellent suggestion that we have students annotate our syllabi. I stopped thinking of my syllabus as a finished document and stopped going over it in class on the first day. Instead, I started asking students to annotate the syllabus as their first homework assignment each term.[26] Here's a sample set of instructions for this exercise from when I last taught online: "Make a copy of the course syllabus (linked below) and annotate it. To annotate simply means to take notes, and it's a skill that will be very helpful in this course. Read through the syllabus and add comments—what do you like and why? What are your concerns? What needs clarifying? Have this ready to talk about in class on Friday."

Whether I was teaching in the same physical space as my students or meeting them online, I began the next class period asking students to share their annotations. Sometimes these were simply observations—perhaps someone hadn't seen information about basic needs in the syllabus before, for example—but most of the time the students had questions. Answering these questions helped me identify where my language was opaque or I had assumed a familiarity with academic processes that my students didn't possess. I would take notes on a paper copy of the syllabus and often refine language with my students' help, then go away and edit our shared Google Doc to reflect our conversation. (If you're more mentally, physically, and technologically dexterous than I am, you might pull up an electronic or online version of the syllabus and make the edits in real time.) The result was a document that spoke to our collective priorities, the unique makeup of the class, and a body of students who had paid deep attention to everything on the syllabus.

Wake Forest University has devised another wonderful approach: the academic coaches in the Center for Learning, Access, and Student Success have launched a comprehensive syllabus project. Coaches help students fill out a spreadsheet template each semester where they keep track of every homework assignment, major assessment, or other deadline for each of their courses. This makes for a one-stop guide to help students manage their time, and as Ashley Mowreader reported for Inside Higher Ed, "the exercise encourages students to read their syllabus and learn course expectations."[27] This would be a great exercise to undertake in any number of courses but particularly those tied to the first-year experience. Such a spreadsheet could also be offered by an individual instructor using the Generic Syllabus Maker at Rice University to quickly and easily generate semester dates.[28]

A syllabus is many things. It's an introduction to you for your students—to the way you think, to the things you value about both teaching and your discipline, and to the way you communicate. It's a compass that will help your students navigate the terrain of their learning in your class and hopefully get them back on track if they get lost. It can be a document that suggests you are the singular authority in the classroom, and it can be one that communicates that you think of your students as your collaborators. It is a letter, a map, and a means by which people organize time. Because of all of this, it is one of the most complex documents we will ever write, demanding concerted, generous thinking from us if we want it to do its job. Kindness helps us rethink our syllabi and to craft them as invitations to step into new worlds.

3

KINDNESS AND ASSESSMENT

For many years, I asked students in my intermediate-level history classes to write a research paper as their second major assignment of the term. I told students to think of a topic connected to the course that really interested them, come up with a question related to that topic, do research to formulate an answer to their question, and write up their conclusions. I expected that these papers would be eight to ten pages long. I trusted that my students could intuit my meaning when I said "Do research" or "Write a paper," but I did not spend a lot of time in class exploring those concepts. Instead, I simply included a lengthy list of directions on my assignment sheet to make up for the proactive work I should have done.

In the classes I teach now, my students and I discuss what it means to have "enough" evidence to make a claim—a goalpost that is always moving in history, depending on the time period we're studying, the availability of textual sources in languages students can read, the material and oral sources ethically accessible to us, and the theories of analysis we employ. In years past I simply directed students to an arbitrary number of sources they might use, betraying my distrust that students would only search the web:

As you identify the texts you will use to research the question you've set for yourself, bear in mind that you should include in your tally:

(1) no more than two secondary-source websites
(2) at least six scholarly articles
(3) at least two books

The assignment sheet I wrote had to do a lot of heavy lifting. I assumed someone else was teaching my students how to write good papers, so I didn't need to. Instead, I included a checklist of things my students should consider before turning in their essay. That I cared about these things would have been brand-new information:

- Your paper should have a thesis statement that appears in your introductory paragraph. Each successive paragraph should help build an argument in support of your thesis. Your paper must also have a conclusion.
- It is a good idea to follow the rule of one idea per paragraph. Each paragraph should develop that idea with evidence—a one or two sentence paragraph is therefore not developed. A paragraph that runs for most of a page probably contains too many ideas.
- Cite your sources carefully, using footnotes or endnotes that follow the rules set out in *The Chicago Manual of Style*. (The quick guide is under the "About" section of Classroom.) Include a bibliography at the end of your paper.
- Use 12-point font (the size you see on this assignment sheet).
- Your essay must be double-spaced and have one-inch margins.

The problem here was not the provision of structure, which is an important part of learning. The problem was that I assumed too much and did too little: I thought that unless I told them otherwise, students would turn in papers with wildly inflated fonts, extra padding in the margins, extra spaces between the lines, and that, in general, they would write badly. Small wonder, then, that I grew frustrated when my students couldn't read my mind, and my students ended up frustrated as they tried to show me that they could research, read critically, and analyze texts.

Assessments of all kinds are a point of inquiry into student learning on the part of instructors, but the details of what we're asking vary wildly across disciplines and also across our intellectual commitments to certain kinds of thinking about learning, failure, and success. When I had my students write papers, I thought I was asking, *What did you learn in the last four weeks of this course?* Instead, I came to realize I was asking, *Can you write according to some unarticulated specifications I have about that medium, and do so clearly enough that I can tell what you know?* Likewise, when, as a brand-new professor, I asked students to write book reviews in the style of particular history journals, I thought I was asking, *Did you understand the book you read?* Instead, in time, I came to realize I was asking, *Do you understand how to do a very specific part of an advanced historian's job?*

My assignments were an example of the constrained thinking that so often accumulates like dust around assessment activities. I had not asked myself what I needed to do to make sure my students could show me their learning because I simply replicated the ways in which I had been taught. Academia has a long history of neglecting to share important information with students: no one ever taught me how to write a history essay, so it didn't occur to me it was a thing you *could*—and *should*—be taught. If there was learning to be done, I assumed it would come after the assignment was completed and graded, when students pored over my comments and corrections and internalized them. (Oh, the hubris!)

Giving serious thought to how we're asking students to show us what they know is a kindness. There's a difference between being asked to craft an essay about color theory in an art history class and showing an understanding of color theory in a studio painting class. While both the essay and the painting demonstrate knowledge, the medium for expressing that knowledge can close doors for some students as much as open them for others. A music student might easily express their understanding of scales and arpeggios on a piano but be wholly unable to do the same on a trombone. They still understand what a scale is. This holds true outside the arts and humanities too. It is, for example, possible for a student to show an instructor that they know how to conduct a particular chemistry experiment in real time while finding it challenging to write that knowledge down mathematically. As Clarissa Sorensen-Unruh, a faculty member in chemistry at Central New Mexico Community College, puts it, "Math is its own language, and speaking English or even laboratory chemistry doesn't mean you speak math well."[1]

So, what questions are we asking our students when we construct our assignments? Which questions are articulated clearly and directly, and which are implied? Which allow students to demonstrate their authentic learning, and which do not? Which methods of assessment place obstacles in the way of a student's expression of knowledge? If a particular medium of communication is necessary for our discipline, do we spend as much time teaching that medium—that language—as we do the content of our class so that students can succeed at both knowing things and telling us what they know about those things in the manner we need? Is what we understand to be a need something unequivocal and necessary or simply the way we were taught? A pedagogy of kindness challenges us to answer these questions honestly and to break out of our constrained thinking about assessment to create something vibrant, trusting, and new.

The Hidden Curriculum

The first question too many assessments ask is implicit: *Are you good enough?* This question is the foundation of every gatekeeping course: the course where the instructor is proud of the number of Ds and Fs that they hand out; the course graded on an implacable curve; the course where an instructor is not interested in overall student success but only in the success of those students they think belong. That belonging is often rooted in the ability to understand a dense text, or a work of art, or a set of equations easily. It's about a student's ability to intuit what to do and when. It's about a set of presumptions about who should be in college, and it shows little to no regard for first-generation students, students entering college from under-resourced schools, students encountering information for the first time, students with disabilities, students who don't share key identities with the instructor, or students for whom the dominant classroom language—be it English, mathematics, or a minor scale—is new. It is, as Jordynn Jack and Viji Sathy describe it, "a hidden curriculum."[2]

"Rigor" is often the word behind which these practices hide. Notoriously ill-defined, rigor is often rhetorically positioned in opposition to courses where anything goes. As sociologist Deborah Cohan writes, reflecting on what she perceives to be a lack of rigor in pandemic-era instruction, non-rigorous courses are those where educators "refuse to assign grades of D and F and sometimes even the C range, who have no penalties for late work, who allow endless revisions, who will meet their students virtually in the evenings and on weekends, and who readily offer incompletes as a solution—even when a student has done virtually nothing all semester." Cohan offers no context in which the pedagogical choices she lists could be defensible, instead implying they are across-the-board rules employed by instructors who can be summed up as the "grace and compassion police." Such instructors are, she argues, involved in a "shame-blame game," leaving their colleagues "feel[ing] never good enough." Physicist David Syphers agrees, suggesting that rigor is most at home in the sciences but could be found in the humanities, provided that instructors—like his former professor—didn't hand out A grades "like candy or pretend like there are no consequences in life for substandard work."[3]

Certainly, the pandemic destabilized the way in which many instructors approached teaching, requiring that everyone involved in higher ed make rapid adaptations to new modalities of learning. But teaching does not occur in a vacuum; it never has. Our students are not brains in a jar but fully realized human beings with multiple claims upon their time, energy, and resources—emotional, physical, and financial. The pandemic has joltingly demanded that we all see our students within the context of their full lives—that we take their trauma into account; that we think clearly about the risks to their health; that we give them time to recover from being sick and to grieve; that we consider the explosive ramifications of the digital divide; that we figure out how to offer resources to students scattered in different time zones without access to the library; that we teach students whose learning space is the kitchen, shared with family and friends, or the break room at their job. But here's the key: we should have always had these considerations—wellness, illness, grief, access, resources, money, time—in mind. And our job is not simply to teach content but to teach people. That requires inventive thinking about how to meet our students in the messy circumstances of their lives, just as they meet us in the messy circumstances of ours.

As Jack and Sathy put it, teaching should not be "an obstacle race . . . [where you], as the instructor, set up the tasks and each student has to finish them (or not) to a certain standard and within a set time . . . [and if] only a few students can do it, that means the course is rigorous."[4] Teaching is not at its best when it breaks students and tells them they'll fail, but rather when it's about collaborating with students to define and embody success. How much richer would our teaching lives be if we did not imagine ourselves to be holding the line against "out-of-place" students and instead considered ourselves as succeeding when they do too? There are students who may not meet the requirements of a given class, and I'm not here to suggest that a pedagogy of kindness means there are never consequences for actions. Some students may indeed fail a course. But those Fs (and Ds) are not a badge of honor for an instructor but rather instructive: something, somewhere, went wrong.

Confronting Ableism

A great deal of what we assume about undergraduate learning and assessment is (sometimes completely unwittingly) rooted in ableism. For example, my undergraduate and graduate professors taught me that historians communicate through writing—that the act of writing is inseparable from the act of knowing. But this is plainly untrue. Writing has certainly been one of the most important methods for communicating academic knowledge in Western systems of higher education for centuries.[5] But because of this, many historians have conflated writing, analysis, and the making of meaning, as if those things could not happen in other ways. It has taken academia years—and it is an ongoing process—to reveal people's assumptions about who gets to participate in academic spaces based on the expectation that knowledge should be written down. Many communities have knowledge of time, space, place, and history that have been passed down, critically examined, and found necessary and meaningful as oral bodies of information. Not all that information is owed to every person; there are limits on what might be told within certain communities and outside of them.[6] Yet that knowledge is still historical, and its existence should cause historians to rethink and reshape the traditional definition of our fields to encompass multiple ways of knowing and expressing that knowledge. And despite those naysayers who still insist that writing is more trustworthy than oral communication, even the stuffiest, most traditional academic historians talk. They gather in small communities and large ones to discuss meaning; over time they have created seminars, lectures, and conference panels in order to tell others their thoughts. The association between writing and historical knowledge is not a natural phenomenon but a construction.[7] It can be deconstructed. There is no need to insist that my students limit themselves to the written word in showing me what they know.

When I require nothing but writing from my students, that choice is not just an expression of cultural hegemony but one of academic ableism. Academia has always been ableist. Learning was, until very recently, something that happened on a brick-and-mortar campus that was rarely designed to allow access to individuals with physical disabilities. The expansion of higher education in the late nineteenth and early twentieth centuries ran alongside (and drew upon) eugenicist thinking that marginalized and often physically harmed individuals with mental illnesses, neurocognitive differences, and behaviors (like sexual expression) that ran afoul of dominant narratives about purity and worth.[8] We have not shaken off the dirt that clings to these roots. This is not just a matter of who is admitted to our institutions, or who can move easily through physical academic spaces; it expresses itself through the subtleties of our disciplinary expectations. If, for example, we insist that students must demonstrate their understanding of concepts, principles, and ideas through writing alone, we risk marginalizing and alienating students whose disabilities make it difficult to express themselves through that medium and organize words on a page. It is vital that we distinguish between the substance we hope our students know and the means by which they tell us they know it as part of a concerted effort to undo ableist practices.

Educators are frequently called upon to mitigate (although not transform) ableism through accommodations, and almost every instructor has experience with such requests. Nevertheless, many educators are unclear about them, have been misinformed as to what a notification of a student accommodation means, or are sometimes just plain prejudiced against students with disabilities.[9] Accommodations are a matter of law. College and universities in the United States, for example, are subject to the regulations contained in the Americans with Disabilities Act (ADA). Title II of the act says: "No qualified individual with a disability shall, on the basis of disability, be excluded from participation in or be denied the benefits of the services, programs, or activities of a public entity, or be subjected to discrimination by any public entity." Colleges and universities—by virtue of their funding mechanisms—are public entities, and must therefore "make reasonable modifications in policies, practices, or procedures," to ensure that individuals with disabilities are not discriminated against.[10] Accommodations—changes to "policies, practices, or procedures" both in and out of the classroom—ensure that individuals with disabilities have access to the same quality of education as people who aren't disabled.

But for someone to qualify for an accommodation, their disability has to be documented. This means turning in expensive testing or medical information to the office of disability services (called by different names on different campuses) where someone—hopefully an expert—decides which accommodations a student should receive. That decision is communicated to faculty and staff and it is the law that they follow that directive. Yet there is an insidious idea among some educators that if a student cannot do what many other students do—such as take an exam without notes in an environment that may be noisy or distracting—they're gaming the system, getting away with something that they shouldn't get away with. The implicit assumption is that there's a "right" way—normative, neurotypical—to do college, and that any deviation from that way is wrong.

The way that many people do college is predicated upon physical and mental ability: the liberty to move around easily, to have a reasonable supply of energy each day, to be free from lasting pain, to be able to easily organize one's thoughts, to moderate sensory input, to distinguish between real threats to the self and threats that seem real because of psychological conditioning, for example. But not everyone has access to these things, and believing otherwise marginalizes people who need assistive devices, or experience serious medical side effects, or who are schizophrenic, or have dyscalculia (to name a handful of the many, many reasons someone might qualify for accommodations).[11] People with disabilities are no less creative, capable, thoughtful, talented, or analytical than anyone else—but insisting that all students communicate, act, move, and think as if they are not disabled denies disabled people's reality. Many people who consider themselves abled know this to some degree: they would agree that having ramps to get into campus buildings is a fair accommodation for someone who is in a wheelchair (and benefit from ramps when they are, say, tired or pushing a stroller).[12] But when it comes to other accommodations, people lose the clarity they might have about ramps and become suspicious that a student is gaining some kind of unfair advantage over their peers.[13]

Even at its best, the accommodation system provides a hit-and-miss response to the needs of students with disabilities. Being able to provide the documentation necessary to get an accommodation requires being an advocate for oneself, even in instances where a disability may make energy a scarce resource. It requires access to medical professionals who take a person seriously; money for—and transportation to—testing; and often a good working knowledge of the possibilities an institution may consider in response to a request. It also requires that we—faculty, staff, and students—know that we are disabled, which is not a given. For example, the symptoms of ADHD most easily recognizable to medical professionals are those that commonly manifest in white boys and men, who have been the subject of the greatest number of research studies. Women and genderqueer people of all races, as well as men of color, may not recognize that they have ADHD or have a medical professional recognize it in them.[14] Many people with ADHD spend years thinking they are disorganized or lazy.[15] This means students may not know what to be tested for or to ask for accommodations.

We must therefore learn to teach in ways that welcome the diversity of students' bodies and minds. One way to do this is to deploy Universal Design for Learning (UDL) to compassionately increase the accessibility of our courses. UDL is a framework for thinking about course design that prioritizes accessibility across multiple axes, including disability, and which values flexibility and choice for both instructors and students alike. (Like the ramp on a building that serves people pushing strollers as well as people in wheelchairs, it allows multiple groups of people greater access to learning.) Put most simply, rather than waiting to find out which students need particular support by waiting for an accommodation notice that may never arrive, UDL practitioners design their courses to embrace multiple points of access into course materials and multiple methods of inquiry, learning, and assessment. "UDL posits that designing for learner variability ahead of time—before instructors even know their students—is the most effective way to reduce individual accommodation needs," write Thomas J. Tobin and Kirsten T. Behling.[16] Such an approach does not require a sixth sense about any single incoming class but instead a recognition of some common needs among our students. Take the syllabus I discussed in the last chapter, for example. I make that syllabus available in both a hard copy that students can write on, fold, and file and an electronic copy that they can enlarge, duplicate, and annotate if they wish. I include headers and icons on my syllabus for students who find it difficult to parse large blocks of text, and I embed alt text in those images for students who use screen readers to access that information. Providing options for how students interact with that key piece of course infrastructure means that I can reach students who have reading disabilities, who experience challenges with focus, and who have different preferences about taking notes without anyone having to disclose those needs. It also means my course materials will reach students who do not have the knowledge, money, time, energy, or desire to secure accommodations.

UDL can sometimes sound overwhelming: How can we possibly know and provide for the many different challenges our students face in approaching learning in our class? But applying UDL does not mean that we are asked to be soothsayers or that we immediately need to tear everything to pieces and create our courses anew. Tobin and Behling suggest that UDL "is an iterative process, where you and your colleagues create progressively more course content and interactions to be increasingly more accessible as you teach the course repeatedly." Put another way, UDL is "plus-one thinking about the interactions in your course. Is there just one more way that you can help keep learners on task, just one more way that you could give them information, just one more way that they could demonstrate their skills?"[17] Where assessments are concerned, there are multiple ways in which we can practice "plus one." Instead of requiring that students write a paper, for example, we can also give students the opportunity to make a short audio recording (with transcript) or video (with captions; we should be modeling the necessity of access in all things, and instructors are often disabled too). Recordings can be done by Zoom or an app on a student's phone so that no special effects or sound/video editing are required. Instead of writing out our feedback on an assessment, we can ourselves record our thoughts in a two- or three-minute audio clip.[18] There are excellent books on UDL that offer concrete advice about ways to incorporate UDL into our teaching in sustainable ways, as well as CAST's online UDL guidelines, which help an instructor target certain challenges they face in class, identify solutions, and read the research that informs that advice.[19]

It's important to note that shifting to a UDL framework does not do away with the presence or necessity of accommodations altogether. None of us can anticipate every need a student may have, nor can we design the "perfect" class in which every conceivable accommodation is built in. UDL is not magic but rather a holistic approach to education that benefits everyone. The breadth of student needs that require accommodations can and will change with time; so will innovations in assuring access. Our teaching will never and should never reach some point of stasis where we no longer need to think creatively about our classrooms, our students, the content we teach, our own needs, and accessibility.

So, what does this look like on the ground? How do we, as instructors, get honest with ourselves about what our assignments are asking students to do, think critically about whether that's what we *actually* want students to do, and provide flexibility for them to demonstrate their learning moving forward? How do we take that core principle of a pedagogy of kindness—believing in our students—and apply it the way we assess our students work?

Here's one example. In my entry-level history courses I used to give quizzes that focused on primary-source analysis. We spent several class periods honing our analytical skills together and learning the SOCC (Source, Observe, Contextualize, and Corroborate) framework for processing evidence from the past. On quiz day, I would distribute a source that my students hadn't seen previously and give them around thirty minutes to analyze it. This, I came to realize, had numerous drawbacks for students with disabilities. Many students needed extra time for the quiz, which meant putting them in a separate room so that they had a distraction-free testing environment but which also meant they would miss part of the class discussion that came after the quiz. Students with anxiety felt enormous pressure under the time crunch of in-class work. And while the classroom was quiet during the quiz, this was an incredibly challenging environment for students with ADHD or other cognitive problems: having white noise, or background music, or a podcast playing in the background was vital to their ability to focus.

I made changes. The quizzes became a take-home assignment, and I gave students twenty-four hours to complete the quiz. My assumption was still that it was an assessment that would take thirty to forty-five minutes, but my students could choose when they did it and under what environmental conditions. I also made the quiz open note. While I had previously guarded against this, thinking it was an easy path toward cheating, I ultimately realized that I wanted my students to be able to apply prior knowledge as they analyzed their source and to learn how to critically search for answers when they didn't have them. The result was not rampant plagiarism but rather better responses to the quiz. Students analyzed their source more deeply and had the time to notice things they might previously have missed. They also became more thoughtful web users, taking the time to assess the trustworthiness of a website rather than heading right to History.com. The improvements were iterative: I learned, too, and built the development of media literacy into my course.

In another example I ultimately scrapped the assignment I described at the beginning of this chapter and chose the "unessay" as one way to resolve the problems my previous assessment practices had created. The unessay was originally dreamed up by Daniel Paul O'Donnell and had a simple goal: "to undo the damage done by [traditional approaches] to teaching writing. It works by throwing out all the rules you have learned about essay writing in the course of your primary, secondary, and post-secondary education and asks you to focus instead solely on your intellectual interests and passions. In an unessay you choose your own topic, present it any way you please, and are evaluated on how compelling and effective you are."[20] I gave the idea some serious thought and wrote the instructions for my own version of the unessay like this:

> Your second assignment is to **show me what you've learned this term** in any medium BUT a paper. That means you could create art, photography, music, dance, poetry, rap, a map, a zine . . . the sky is the limit. Think about what skills you have that you can bring to this assignment!
>
> - You should propose the topic you'd like to research in a one-page Google Doc by Monday, April 25.
> - In that proposal, you should also tell me what you will create.
> - You will create your project and bring it to class on Monday, May 16. You'll also submit a 3–5 page reflection that tells me what you learned by completing your project, and a bibliography.

This unessay project was designed so that students could show me what they knew using a fresh medium. While I did allow students the option to write traditional papers the first few times I made an unessay assignment, it quickly became clear that papers constituted a safe choice for my students rather than one that would foster the greatest expression of their learning. It was familiar; it did not ask my students to grow. Instead, I worked with my students to help them identify a new way to communicate their ideas in concert with a more informal, reflective essay at the project's end. (Your mileage on whether to include a formal paper option in an unessay assessment may vary; your discipline's may too.)

The students who've completed unessays in my classes have done the most incredible work: researched and cooked food that is native to the Americas, embroidered samplers with critiques of nineteenth-century womanhood, created entirely new board games to demonstrate how difficult it is for Native nations to gain federal recognition, written screenplays about gay pirates, built 3D maps of queer neighborhoods in turn-of-the-century New York City, thrown pots in which to keep the metaphorical ashes of coverture (the web of laws which governed the relationship between husbands and wives), coded computer games to allow people to think through settler colonialism, and created folders of blackout poetry about heteronormativity. All of these projects were accompanied by in-depth research and metacognitive reflective pieces that showed me a student's skill acquisition and critical thought.

And this is about accessibility. Here, accessibility means, in very definite terms, allowing students to work in the medium that will allow them to communicate their learning, following the principles of UDL. But the assignment is about many other kinds of access, too: access to cultural memory and knowledge; access to researching a topic that is personally meaningful; access to peer support and problem-solving; access to time to dive into liberatory theories about race, class, gender, sexuality, religion, and more. This is key.

The unessay is just one example of a solution to the problem of constrained thinking around assignments. It's not only for history classes, although I have benefited from the creativity and guidance of some incredible history instructors as I've refined my approach.[71] I also look to other educators for examples. Clarissa Sorensen-Unruh has her chemistry students fill out learning journals in which, five times a semester, they make connections between what they're learning in class and the wider world. The journals can be written, but Sorensen-Unruh also welcomes "concept maps, videos, [and] infographics . . . I told them if they wanted to TikTok their learning journals, I was cool with it." This dismantles barriers between students and their learning and allows them to show their thinking in the way that's best for them. Every instructor I know is deeply invested in learning what their students understand, extrapolate, and infer about both content and skills, and the unessay (or unjournal) is one way in which we can make it easier to both inquire *What do you know?* and make the playing field as level as possible when it comes to formulating an answer.

Grading, Ungrading, and Feedback

Just as we must reflect on what explicit and implicit questions we are asking our students in the design of our assessment activities, we must ask ourselves similarly important questions regarding the way we do or do not grade. The idea of not grading may seem puzzling to some; after all, with few notable exceptions, most institutions of higher ed require that educators turn in final grades for students at the end of each semester, quarter, or term. But how do we get to that final grade? Have we asked ourselves what function grades perform in our courses? Do they support learning or frustrate it? And why do grades matter to us? Do they represent, as Munir Fasheh argues, a way for us to encourage "control, winning, profit, individualism and competition"?[22] Are they used to shame people? Can they, in contrast, be used to build them up and affirm their growth? Can grades be about joy?[23]

For the entirety of my career as an educator, grading would have come absolutely last in any ranking I could make of the activities associated with my job. I was never taught how to grade. In my first semester as a teaching assistant, I was tasked with grading ID quizzes—quizzes where students were provided with key terms from the course and had to correctly define them and explain their significance. I carefully considered what an ideal answer would be for each one and assigned point values to each component part. I then sailed into grading and docked points for everything a student missed. No one had explained that, in the humanities, numerical grades often stand in as placeholders for letter grades: if someone earns a C, that's worth 75 out of 100 points—not because there are twenty-five things someone missed, but because someone, somewhere, at some point, decided that 70 to 80 points represented C-level work. I graded, I docked points, and then realized everyone in the class had failed or earned a D despite demonstrating they understood the larger themes of the class. It took a while for me to straighten out what had happened and adjust my grading accordingly. And once I did adopt what we might call representational grading, I spent hours trying to figure out if someone had a B-plus that was worth 88 points or 89. I was told this was just how things were done; there was no internal logic to the system that anyone could explain beyond "tradition."[24] (And the United Kingdom had its own representational system where a 70 was a "first," not a C minus, so I was especially confused.)

My experience is illustrative of something at the heart of all grading systems: they depend on individual interpretations of a students' work and, as such, are inconsistent. Even when instructors are teaching very similar courses within a field, they may not agree on what a C is. They may also apportion grades differently, with one deciding 30 percent of a course grade is from attendance while the other prefers 15 percent, for example, or 50 percent of the grade comes from quizzes, while another instructor prefers 40 percent. Then there are the differences between fields. How do we compare a biology exam to a piece of literary criticism? If a student is permitted one attempt to apply an algebraic equation but many attempts to draft a history paper, how can they earn the same grade? A timed in-class essay will yield different results from a take-home quiz. And yet almost everyone must use the letters A to D (plus F) to represent a student's relative success in any class. There is almost no consistency within departments or across campuses, and there are thousands of campuses across the United States.[25] One might argue that negotiating this inconsistency is one of the skills a student develops in college, fine-tuning their work to meet the expectations of dozens of individual instructors. If that is the case, it is incumbent upon us to tell students this directly and teach them how to do it as well as communicate it to GPA-conscious employers beyond campus too.

Grades are complicated, not least because they are a proxy for a host of feelings about belonging, not belonging, success, failure, and choice. To one student they might represent the extrinsic motivation they need to organize their time and do well on a project, paper, or test.[26] For another, they might generate paralyzing anxiety. For one educator, they might provide a clear way to provide feedback to four hundred students when there's no time to do more. For another, they may represent something that feels crushingly antithetical to what they became an educator to do.

For me, grading was something that I poured hours into without feeling like I was seeing a return. I often saw evidence that, as Jeffrey Schinske and Kimberley Tanner have argued, "grades can dampen existing intrinsic motivation, give rise to extrinsic motivation, enhance fear of failure, reduce interest, decrease enjoyment in class work, increase anxiety, hamper performance on follow-up tasks, stimulate avoidance of challenging tasks, and heighten competitiveness." I discovered that while getting a high grade often motivated students to work toward earning another high grade, getting a low grade usually discouraged their growth. I also learned that even when educators included good counsel and comments alongside letter or number grades, students tended to read the grade but not the longer feedback.[27] Why was I line editing papers? Why was I taking pains to write affirming things next to a letter or number as well as suggesting how students could improve if it didn't make a dent?

What I wanted from my students' assignments, and my responses to them, was to spark a conversation about each person's strengths and an opportunity to think seriously about their past, present, and future growth. I hated being the only person weighing in on these things. I also genuinely dreaded the conversations students might want to have after a paper was returned, and the intellectual cartwheels I felt I had to turn to defend my grading practices. My experiences were not isolated; the conversations I've had with educators across the country suggest we need to do better at teaching educators *how* to grade and to have frank conversations about our hopes, fears, and frustrations with regard to the practice. Grading is another example of something established practitioners frequently assume everyone knows how to do because they were once graded as students. We need to approach the act with greater intentionality.

When I reflected upon my own grading experiences—as both teacher and student—I decided to do less and less grading, course by course, and embrace the concept of "ungrading." There are several definitions of "ungrading" in circulation, but one that resonates with me was offered by Lindsay C. Masland: "For me, ungrading is a *philosophy* of assessment that seeks to decenter grades (i.e., letters or numbers) in the learning process. There are many specific pedagogical practices that can be labeled as reflective of a commitment to this philosophy, but I believe that ungrading cannot and should not be reduced to a set of instructional moves."[28] It's perhaps useful to think of all ungrading approaches through the "un" in ungrading: unpacking, unpicking, and undoing grading assumptions and schemes. As John Warner suggests, "Ungrading is no one thing. It is not a specific approach or set of techniques so much as a mind-set, a recognition that the relationship between evaluation as it traditionally happens in school contexts and the imperatives of learning is complicated, and for many students, those things have been at odds for the bulk of their academic careers."[29] There are colleges, such as Evergreen and Hampshire, that have done away with grades altogether; they exist at the far end of the ungrading spectrum. When I began exploring ungrading, I was still handing out grades several times a term. Ungrading is best thought of as a process as much as a destination, and I had to work out what it might mean for me.[30]

My first foray into ungrading saw me collaboratively build a grading rubric with my students. I had, for a long time, passed out a list of grading guidelines in my classes, but this time I asked students to read and annotate it alongside me, tell me what seemed fair and unfair, and work with me to make the language more transparent. We edited the document together in real time, and only when we reached consensus about each grading category did we adopt it for the course. I also put together a self-evaluation sheet for students to hand in alongside their assessments. The sheet began with simple check-in questions such as "Did you make connections between different readings in class?" and then expanded into open-ended questions like "What new intellectual territory did you explore in this assignment?" These open-ended questions reframed grading; they suggested that assignments *should* be about new intellectual territory, for example, and a process of self-discovery. The last question on the assessment sheet was "Is there anything else I should know?"—offering students an opportunity to tell me things that I might not otherwise know about their process, about challenges they'd faced, or about things they were particularly proud of. The self-evaluations allowed the students to have a voice in grading as a process, reflect upon their personal and intellectual growth, and provide me with vital information to parse out where a student was struggling or had mastered something new.[31]

I also experimented with how I offered feedback. I had always been fond of telling my students—in writing—what they had done well on an assignment, suggesting where they might strengthen their work further, and wrapping up with affirmation of something they should be proud of. But when I turned to the authority on whether that feedback worked—my students themselves—they told me that this approach was colloquially known as the "shit sandwich" and that the positive comments I made were disregarded in favor of focusing on what they had "done wrong." I decided I would experiment with providing feedback in person to address this situation, holding fifteen-minute grading conversations with each of my students rather than writing comments on their work. Fifteen minutes was less time than I had traditionally spent

KINDNESS AND ASSESSMENT 75

writing feedback on a paper, and it redirected grading away from the punitive process my students expected it to be. There is something very, very different about sharing physical space and hearing someone's tone of voice that changes the dynamics of awarding grades. I began each of these conversations by asking students what they thought of their work and affirming the things they had done well. This made it a much easier and more useful way to segue into discussing how they might become stronger writers or analysts on their next assignment.

As I offered feedback about future improvement, I also limited myself to talking about the two biggest things a student could do to make a big difference on their next piece of work. Too much feedback can be absolutely overwhelming to a student—as many of us can recall from the days when our upper-level and graduate work came back from our advisers covered in red ink.[32] Line edits, for example, are not easy to parse when you're learning the rules of clear expression unless they're accompanied by a strong explanation of why the order of certain words is incorrect, or the tense important, or the sentence too long. And whether we're dealing in writing, equations, painting, or dance, it's tempting to want to transform our students' rough work into something that approaches perfection, but that's a daunting task for a student to tackle between one assignment and the next.

Instead I focus on what will have the greatest immediate impact. For some of my students it's spending longer analyzing a primary source. For others it's learning to write a clearer topic sentence, or providing concrete evidence to back up a claim. Until I'm teaching the majors-only classes in my field, it's rarely about split infinitives or dangling participles. If I do need to offer direction on grammar and expression, I do so with the student right there, in conversation, limiting my line editing to one paragraph and explaining why the rules I'm applying exist. (This can be done over Zoom as easily as physically sitting side by side.) Over the course of a semester, quarter, or term, this approach can transform a student's work and, crucially, does not drown them in detail.

I teach at a college where my classes are never more than thirty students in size, and I teach just two classes every trimester, which means I have the time to hold such conversations. But the practice of talking to students is adaptable. I have canceled class for a period or two to make sure I have the time to engage with students; I believe in the approach so deeply that I think it is worth the loss of classroom time. You might also record a short voice memo offering feedback, an approach that humanizes you and makes it much easier for students to parse your genuine enthusiasm and encouragement as well as critique. When you have hundreds of pieces of feedback to wrangle, you might still ask students to self-assess through a written doc or Google form so that they have the opportunity to participate in the process. It takes only a few moments to read these through before writing feedback in return. Each of these approaches emphasizes that we believe in our students: that grading, like so much else in our classrooms, can be intentionally collaborative.

Any one of these changes would have been a great first step in the ungrading process. What was important was that I transformed my grading piece by piece, little by little, giving me time to experiment, to figure out where I needed to tweak my approach, and to listen to student feedback about the transition.[33] By spring 2022, I had reached a point where I no longer graded at all. I provided lots of feedback to students on their various assignments, but students themselves engaged in the metacognitive work of reflecting on their learning at the term's end and making a case for the grade they thought they had earned. In deference to research about students' different perceptions of their own success based on variables like race and racism, class, gender, and cultural background, I reserved the right to raise grades where I thought someone was unduly hard on themselves.[34] In an expression of trust I let go of the right to lower them. So far my approach hasn't been abused.

Ungrading is not just for the humanities. Clarissa Sorensen-Unruh (chemistry) and Gary Chu (mathematics) both employ practices that Chu calls a "learning-assessment-feedback cycle."[35] Students in Sorensen-Unruh's and Chu's classes not only answer assessment questions to their best of their ability but rate their confidence in their responses. After receiving feedback on their answers, students then review their exams to identify what went well and what did not and have the opportunity to revise their work. Students are constantly learning *through* their involvement in the grading process rather than simply having grades imposed upon them.[36] Heather Miceli replaced exams in her general science courses with metacognitive reflections. "I used to give exams in this course, and my reasoning was 'it's a science class, how can you teach science without exams?'" she writes. "Of course, my exams were terribly inequitable. For some of my students, the exams were mostly a review from content they learned in high school, but for others, the content was so beyond what they could comprehend because they lacked the basic knowledge I assumed they would have had. . . . How on earth is an 'objective' exam supposed to measure learning under these conditions?"

Now Miceli has students "reflect independently on the topics each week . . . really honing in on how the topics are relevant to their lives" and asks students to self-assess their learning at the end of the course. "My students will tell you that they've learned more in my class than any science class they've taken," she writes.[37]

Some educators are wary about ungrading. As I've worked with different campus communities around the country, I've often heard faculty articulate the concern that without a grade to motivate them, students will not do the work they're assigned, and that this problem has grown worse over the course of the pandemic. While this is often discussed as a question of student disengagement, I think it is perhaps better to frame what's happening as the result of a seismic shift in higher ed.[38] The pandemic has overloaded everyone—cognitively, emotionally, mentally, perhaps even financially—from students to administrators to faculty and staff. While it is wholly understandable to wish this were not the case, there is no going back to what we had before.[39] The pandemic has done more than make us ill, grief-stricken, and overloaded; it has prompted people to reconsider their relationship to work, to office spaces, to education, and to life goals.[40] Now more than ever, we cannot rely on our own belief that our disciplines are full of useful and worthy information and automatically expect students to agree and find meaning in our assignments. As they juggle enormous and multivarious pressures—over and above their personal preference for certain fields over others—students may not see the importance of a given subject or the point of a particular assignment, or have the time to devote to schoolwork at the level we might hope. We must take a hard look at what we're asking students to do and then identify if there is value in it. If there is not, we need to change our assessments. If there is, we need to be able to explain that value to students as clearly and directly as we can.

One way to do this is through the transparent assignment, an approach advocated by Mary-Ann Winkelmes. There are three principles at the heart of this approach: to explain the purpose of an assignment to students, to delineate the task(s) students must complete, and to make the criteria by which they will be evaluated crystal clear. The Transparency in Learning and Teaching (TILT) in Higher Ed website offers multiple models of what such assignments might look like in different disciplines, from sociology to criminal justice, calculus, and political science.[41] I learned about transparent assignment design from my colleague Mary Armon, a professor of mathematics. Here's the beginning of one of her assignments on applications of the integral:

Purpose of this assignment: To learn some more about applications of the integral in "real life" and to practice reporting out results using computations, graphs and paragraphs.

What to do: The calculus in each of these applications is not hard, but understanding the situations might require some time and thought. Please feel free to ask me questions; you shouldn't be talking to anyone else about this work. Your only other resources should be:

- Desmos, Mathematica, Google Sheets, and/or Excel
- the resources linked on Moodle
- your class notes
- the textbook
- the resources linked in Part 2.

If you aren't sure whether or not a resource is allowed, please ask! Please write up your results on paper as legibly as you can; scan to pdf and upload on Moodle. Include explanations in complete sentences. See Grading Criteria below for expectations.

Here's an example of TILT from my own classes: a final assignment from a course where the students and I had spent the term analyzing the 2020 presidential election:

Purpose:

This assignment is designed to

1. Apply your understanding of the importance of historical context
2. Accurately identify the arguments other people are making
3. Make an argument of your own
4. Use sources as evidence
5. Cite sources in a way that allows others to find those sources for themselves.

Task:

For this assignment you must choose a speech President Trump has given since the election, explain the argument he's making, and place it into the larger context of what we've studied in this class. Pay attention to considerations of race, gender, class, religion, ability, and LGBTQ issues.

If I were to revise this assignment now, I might rewrite the purpose statement to include ideas about the meaning of doing this work and its connection to my students' lives, as well as the historical-thinking skills I hoped they would demonstrate. Even better, I might ask my students to discern the purpose of the assignment for themselves and create their own meaning from the project. While this assignment sheet was accompanied by a copy of my department's rubric for assessing essays as a means of demystifying my grading expectations, I would also likely now ask students to create a rubric together, addressing not only the application of course content and historical skills but the value of the assignment to their learning overall.

There are other ways to affirm the importance of the particular kind of learning we're asking students to do. In the past I had students keep journals in which they recorded their thoughts about the assigned readings and had them graded several times a term. This was labor-intensive work for all of us and very much an assignment that was designed to pressure students to read rather than giving them a good reason to do so. Now I have my students complete a five-question reading reflection through a Google form after almost every reading. Question one asks students to report in on how much of the assigned reading they've done through radio button options: None; between 1 percent and 25 percent; between 26 percent and 50 percent; between 50 percent and 100 percent; or all of the assigned reading. I make it clear to my students that this is a question I'm asking not to be punitive but simply so that when I walk into the classroom on any given day I know how best to meet my students where they are. I then ask:

2. What new things did you learn from the reading?
3. What do you think it's important we talk about today?
4. What left you confused? What questions do you have?
5. Is there anything else you want to share?

I do not grade these reflections. Students do not get a direct response from me unless they have shared something in question number five that requires a follow-up: a roommate situation, illness, worry, hunger. But I take their responses and I work them into my lesson plans for each class period, specifically addressing the questions they've asked and concentrating on areas they found interesting and/or confusing. This establishes a feedback loop; my students see that their responses have value and that they are helping to co-create the course.

This is another example of ungrading but also an example of providing students with structure. All assessment activities in my classes—the reading reflections; metacognitive reflections on the previous week's learning before a new one begins; lessons on navigating the library; classes where we analyze websites; paper workshops; unessays; citations—offer structure to the work of learning and have deadlines attached.[42] Students in my courses are always allowed extensions, no questions asked, but deadlines help all of us pace our work and keep us focused, and build upon conversations and resources related to organization and time management shared at the beginning of term. (I once experimented with omitting deadlines altogether and must give a shout-out to alums who wrote two papers in one night for The History of Birth Control and Reproduction in winter 2013. I learned that both my students and I needed structure in place if learning was to happen.) Structure and choice can happily coexist.

We can believe in our students and collaborate on any number of different grading systems.[43] What's key, whether we affix numbers and letters to the end of assessments or not, is to honestly grapple with the pros and cons of those systems for students of all abilities and backgrounds, and to be able to defend our practices on the basis of reasoning that reaches far beyond the fallback position of "tradition." As Viji Sathy and Kelly A. Hogan suggest, one of the most important questions we must ask ourselves when designing our courses is "who might be left behind"?[44] Compassionate pedagogy demands the courses we design reach every student and that we understand not only what implicit and explicit questions we are asking our students but why we believe those questions must be asked at all.

Education is about inquiry. We hope to foster curiosity in students, to have both our questions and their own drive the trajectory of their learning. Curiosity and questions are no less important to us as educators: we must know why we are asking particular kinds of academic labor from our students and ourselves and where and how that labor can be shared. This is not about undermining our expertise and our long years of training but about believing our students can be served by being drawn into the metacognitive work of knowing why and how they're learning as they are. Our choices about assessment activities, including grades, must be choices we can explain candidly to the students they will most affect. And when we ask ourselves a question we cannot answer . . . well, that's a learning experience too.

4

KINDNESS IN
THE CLASSROOM

For years, right before I had to walk into a classroom to teach, I would feel overwhelmed by both nerves and exhaustion. I would consider the energy I'd be required to expend in class and feel wholly ill-equipped to do so. I would worry about whether I was prepared enough, no matter how much time I had invested in that work, and I felt certain that students would have questions I wouldn't be able to answer. For a long time I thought this was imposter syndrome: that I didn't believe I was actually qualified to teach and would be found out by someone, somehow. Part of it was. But now I realize that the greater share of what I felt was based on the assumptions I'd been socialized to adopt about both teaching and students. I anticipated conflict; I thought my students' default was to be suspicious of me and everything I brought to the table. In truth, I was suspicious of *them*, and—without a foundation of trust between us—I resigned myself daily to brace for the worst.

Classrooms do not have to be battlefields. This doesn't mean there aren't times where real conflict will arise in the physical space or Zoom room or discussion board that constitutes our classroom. Sometimes that conflict is useful and generative, breaking the polite silence around oppression and exclusion that has been upheld by generations of academics. Sometimes that conflict is in and of itself oppressive and exclusionary, particularly where we are singled out for abuse and derision based on any number of the social identities we possess. But the vast majority of our students are not showing up in our classrooms with a commitment to fighting, judging, or hating us. So often we ready ourselves for confrontation because that's the message we've been absorbing about teaching since we were first oriented to the job. We are often afraid of what feels like contested space.

For some of our students the classroom is exactly that. Too many have not found a welcome or a sense of belonging on our campuses. This does not need to be through overt acts of hatred, although those exist; it can come from us choosing not to see them as they are. My experience as an undergraduate student was one in which my very real needs were ignored by almost everyone who had sway over my studies. My intellectual curiosity about women's history was, for example, met with professorial laughter or rage. My professors dismissed my questions about how to afford the books they assigned as beyond their scope of practice. I was once very sick with a stomach bug on the morning of an end-of-year exam, and my professor sent me to student health. There, I was given Kaopectate and a touch of morphine and made to sit the exam regardless. The people in positions of power at my university seemed to share a singular vision of what "a life of the mind" should be: isolated, disembodied, and dispassionate. My classes were unkind: I moved in spaces where I was judged and found wanting because of my class status, my gender, and the perceived unruliness of my body. That I had feelings about all of this was another demerit against me.

To teach with kindness is to seek to flip all these experiences on their heads and create classroom spaces in which we cultivate trust and belonging. By believing our students and believing *in* our students, we can work alongside them to intentionally develop the conditions under which we all can flourish and be cognizant of our hopes, questions, and fears. We need to get to know our students, facilitate their getting to know us, and make it possible for them to get to know each other, all with healthy boundaries in place. And then we can invite students to participate in a hundred different ways in the creation of their learning, generating something satisfying, challenging, and unique.

Building a Welcome

Creating a welcoming environment in which students can learn takes some planning and intentionality. "Do not assume that saying 'welcome' will mean people feel welcome," write Maha Bali and her colleagues in their discussion of intentionally equitable hospitality (IEH).[1] The theory of IEH, as applied to educational contexts, posits that the instructor of a class is the host of a gathering and must think critically about the welcome their course offers to students all semester long. This means taking stock of the contexts and practices that make students feel invited into a space and those that leave them excluded. Expanding on the idea in *Designing for Care*, Bali and Mia Zamora write:

> The way we gather matters. . . . A class is often a unique entity, with its own chemistry or "personality." It holds particular memories. A class occurs at a particular time in one's life, and it is experienced in a particular place. Learning together holds the potential for unique growth moments, and can be truly transformational if it is tied to a sense of belonging. If a student gains the experience of being included and heard, it makes a critical difference in what kind of learning is possible for all.

IEH requires that instructors are attentive to the social and cultural contexts from which our classroom dynamics draw. "When we wish to practice IEH, we need to continually renew our intentions to notice oppression and injustice and seek to redress them, to iteratively modify and adapt our practices according to the responses and reactions of participants/learners, particularly those who bring marginalized perspectives," write Bali and Zamora.[2] This means more than saying "I'm so glad to meet you" on the first day of class.

If we choose to use a learning management system (LMS), or have one thrust upon us, we can begin to design for hospitality long before the first day of a semester. Just like our syllabi, our LMS pages should be more than a grouping of policies and a list of homework assignments written in suspicious tone. Our choices about what to highlight should communicate that we are invested in a student's whole person, not simply their brain. On my LMS, one of the first things a student sees are a selection of resources that address many of the concerns they are likely to carry into the semester. The adjacent figure shows a sample from one of my Google Classroom sites. Here, I have included resources on time management and self-care as a first port of call in a storm—a place to which students can return when they need the assistance that each resource can provide. Among the self-care resources to which I link are long lists of activities that offer suggestions for multiple kinds of self-care: coloring pages, student zines on self-care principles, and questions we can ask to discern the care we need when we feel nothing is okay.[3] The National Alliance on Mental Illness offers a self-care inventory sheet that allows students to consider the areas in which they might need self-care the most, while the Life Balance wheel allows students take inventory of the physical, financial, intellectual, emotional, social, and spiritual needs they have and draw up a plan for creating individualized

A screenshot from Google Classroom.

stability.[4] I also link to an article by Devon Price about the ways in which people perceive themselves to be lazy and label themselves as such. This is an article to which I regularly refer students when they struggle with procrastination. (Calling ourselves lazy is a reaction to fear, anxiety, and other stressors that have nothing to do with laziness or other "deficits" that students might have self-identified in themselves or been told they possess.) I also offer a link to a Google Chrome extension that can read documents to students if they struggle with processing words on a page.[5] This section grows over time, as I find other resources from which students might benefit.

Beneath "Resources," my students find a section of my LMS clearly labeled "Start Here," offering clear direction for how to interact with the course site. This section includes a link to a video introduction I made about myself, and a transcription of the same. I invite students to watch or read this before I ask them to introduce themselves to me.

Students will then find the syllabus for the course and a space to sign up to engage in a collective note-taking practice where two students per class period volunteer to take notes that will then be uploaded to the LMS. (This practice means that when a student misses class for any reason, or needs to listen without typing or writing—or simply doesn't understand some of our discussion on a given day—there is a support system in place to help them. It also communicates the centrality of community to our endeavors.)

Michelle Pacansky-Brock argues that we should welcome our students by reaching out to them a week before a class begins to make their transition into a course successful. "Pre-course contact is your opportunity to welcome your students, ease their anxieties, make a positive first impression, and ensure they know exactly what they are expected to do that first week and how to do it," she writes.[6] Viji Sathy and Kelly A. Hogan concur. "What information do you not have from campus systems that would better help you to form relationships?" they ask, suggesting that a pre-course survey of students that asks about their unique identities, their past educational experiences, and their ideas about what inclusivity might mean in the classroom can help instructors emphasize belonging and community from the very moment a course begins.[7]

There are, however, good reasons for many of us, especially contingent faculty, to begin work on the first day of our contract and not before. If that describes you, consider sending out a welcome message to all your students early on the first day of class. Tell them you're looking forward to meeting them, make sure they know how and where to congregate—a physical space on your campus? a Zoom room? an LMS discussion board?—and share anything that will help them have a successful first day. Alleviate common anxieties: Specify what they need to have to participate comfortably in class—a laptop? access to a book? just their curiosity?—and give them some idea of what the agenda for the class period will be. This is especially important for those neurodivergent students for whom routines and predictability are key to their success.[8]

It can be a nerve-racking prospect to meet a new cohort of students. It can be a much less fraught moment, however, if we enter it with a spirit of kindness, acknowledging our hopes and our trepidation and keeping in mind that students will be feeling numerous and perhaps conflicting emotions too. If we can grant that everyone is likely a little uncomfortable, we can enter the classroom as a colleague of those arriving to learn, avoiding both the imperative to "be a bitch" as well the feeling of being thrown to the lions. For some instructors, arriving early allows them to tackle their jitters by giving them time to set up slides, projectors, or recordings. It can also provide the opportunity to welcome students as they trickle in or to circulate among them and begin to learn who they are.[9] But while English professor Mary Rose O'Reilley once wrote that some of her colleagues are "conscientious about getting to class early so that they are able to welcome their students," conscientiousness can take myriad forms.[10] For those who can manage it—by temperament or by the grace of a schedule that allows it—being early enough to welcome students is a wonderful act of hospitality. There are those of us, however, whose particular brand of deep introversion or expression of neurodiversity makes it actively painful to stand in front of the classroom as students arrive. I, for example, do much better in providing a welcome if I can enter the classroom right before class begins and offer a genuine greeting to everyone who's assembled before jumping into a class period that is devoted to expanding on a cheerful "Hello!" Where a before-class ritual is not possible—the previous class doesn't get out on time; we're driving between two campuses; the internet goes down—I appreciate O'Reilley's suggestion that we can engage in "graceful leave-taking" at the end of class instead.[11]

Just as we reach out to students to create a welcome, we should encourage them to reach back. For years I passed out a "first day" sheet at the beginning of classes that asked for the name a student wanted me to use for them in class, their pronouns (if they felt comfortable sharing them), and some basic questions about my students' expectations of the course.[12] I asked about their past experience with history classes and if there was anything else I should know that would help me support them during the term. The last question I posed on the handout was "Complete this sentence: I'm the one who . . ."—which always generated deeply unique responses that helped me remember my students' names.[13] During the pandemic, I transferred all these questions to a Google form and added new questions about my students' well-being. I made it very clear that disclosure was not mandatory but asked if anyone was experiencing food insecurity, housing insecurity, or problems securing the technology they needed to participate in an online class. I could then use this information to connect students to the relevant campus offices that could resolve the issue. I also asked if anyone would like me to mail them a fidget toy, which they could select from a list (pre-pandemic, I would bring these to my classroom in a basket) and whether anyone would like a reading strip (a rectangular piece of plastic with a clear window to isolate single lines of text that many students with reading or attention difficulties have found helpful).[14] Each inquiry communicated care, from wanting to correctly calibrate the content of the class to affirming that assistive devices were welcome in the classroom space.

It's an act of welcome, whenever and wherever possible, to learn your students' names. This makes a real difference to the way in which students feel they are perceived. About one-third of the 3,004 students who responded to a recent Inside Higher Ed poll on student success said that they did better in class when their instructor took the time to get to know them, and multiple research studies have concluded that students do better when they and their instructor have a rapport.[15] What that looks like in a large lecture class versus a small seminar is very different, but it's important to prioritize it in whatever way we can. If you can avoid it, do not take roll. Our class lists are often out of date, dead-naming trans, nonbinary, agender, and genderqueer students, and a roll call can out those students without their consent. There are also many other students who go by a name other than their legal name for a host of reasons, and there is little about being misidentified that is welcoming. If you must take attendance, try a Google form or something similar as a means for students to check in, or have students sign a sheet of paper to indicate their presence, or perhaps draw up a seating chart. You can also have students check out of class with a short freewrite on something they learned that day. This metacognitive strategy helps solidify their understanding of their own learning, gives you a way to calibrate your sense of the class period with theirs, and acts as an attendance mechanism.

There are other ways to learn and use our students' names. When I'm teaching in the same physical space as my students, I use department funds to buy sticky name tags that I ask students to wear in class. If your institution doesn't have the money for such a thing, or your class is prohibitively large, consider asking students to make name tents made from a sheet of notepaper to set on their desks. Zoom and other video conferencing apps have made using names easier by placing them in each person's video window, and you can ask students to update that name to their nickname or other chosen name, and to include pronouns if they choose. I also have students introduce one another on the first day of class. Introducing oneself to a room full of new peers can be tremendously anxiety producing for students, so I try to mitigate this by borrowing an activity I learned at the 2017 Digital Pedagogy Lab: I distribute little boxes of Lego figure parts around the class. The boxes contain heads, torsos, and legs, as well as accessories related to a multitude of professions and superhero characters. I pair students up, then ask them to introduce themselves to one another and build a Lego avatar that represents their partner. This gives students something to do with their hands that can bridge awkward pauses and also drives conversation in some unusual directions as each person figures out the best combination of sweaters, pants, handbags, hats, tools, shields, and space lasers to represent someone else. After fifteen minutes we go around the room and the students introduce the avatar they've created. This means we hear each student's chosen name and how to pronounce it correctly, but we displace some of the anxiety in the room by shifting our focus from people to Lego. While in a larger class, where it would quickly become cost-prohibitive to provide enough Lego for two hundred people, partners could draw a representation of an avatar for each other and then introduce that avatar to a small group.[16]

It's important to me that I participate in these activities, both so that I model the curiosity and interest I hope my students will show one another, and so that I do not ask my students to do things I am not prepared to do myself. I also hold part of every first-day class period for students to ask me anything they want. There are some predictable questions: Do I have pets? (Not yet, but I do have three very healthy plants on my living room windowsill that I have managed not to kill.) Why do I like history? (Because as a child I visited a lot of historic houses in Britain and was more or less convinced that if I turned the corner of a hallway quickly enough I would catch people from the past going about their business. Being a historian is still a version of that game.) What was the last thing you watched on TV, or saw on a streaming service, or listened to today? (As of writing, the TV show *Our Flag Means Death* and an Ingrid Michaelson song.) There are always unique questions that I cannot anticipate—about my journey toward being a professor, perhaps, or my thoughts on an item in the news. I answer truthfully, and if I am asked a question I judge as too personal, I gently suggest there are some things I'd like to keep private. I extend the same courtesy to students.

These kinds of activities are often called icebreakers, but my colleague Gabrielle Raley-Karlin calls them warm-ups instead. When we warm up, we're generally growing comfortable, which is a very different association to invoke than the brittle sharpness of breaking ice. Talking to one another is also a muscle to be stretched, just as we might before going on a walk or a run, and it takes practice to do it well. During the pandemic, I asked warm-up questions at the beginning of every class for the whole ten weeks of the term, as it helped us all acclimate to each online synchronous session. I'm a huge fan of "Would you rather . . . ?" questions: Would you rather be able to run faster than the speed of light or fly? Would you rather be a superhero or a sidekick, and why? There are lots of lists of these kinds of questions available online.[17] I also enjoy getting students to think in new directions with questions such as: If you could communicate with anything nonhuman, what would it be? What separates humans from trees? (The last question is a lot harder than it appears when you start to think about it.) There are questions that others have taught me: What's your cure for the common cold? What's your favorite way to eat potatoes? How do you prepare rice? And there's "Tell me a story related to your name," which always elicits wildly varied responses.[18] If you're looking for thought-provoking questions or any number of other warm-up activities, check out those suggested at Equity Unbound's pages online.[19]

As you select your warm-up activities, bear the principles of Universal Design for Learning in mind. Consider how to structure each exercise to make space for students who have high social anxiety, can't make eye contact, or find it hard to follow lengthy verbal instructions, for example. You might mix in verbal responses and written responses to questions, make it clear that you have no particular expectations about body language, and write your instructions on the board or in the chat to reinforce what you're saying out loud. And always design activities with student accommodations in mind so that nothing you ask the whole class to do leaves someone outed against their wishes or feeling alienated by exercises in which they cannot fully participate.

Facilitating a welcoming classroom environment extends beyond the first day, and group work—despite being the subject of many a derisive meme among students and faculty alike—is, when well utilized, a great way to create an atmosphere of belonging. When it comes to this approach, sarah madoka currie is a leader. In her English classes, currie assigns the students to six-person course teams who provide mutual aid for each other throughout the semester. These teams undertake course-related work together every week—assignments that not only build their subject-specific skills but which "build camaraderie . . . [and] trust." One of the first tasks a group undertakes is to "co-design what community-first care looks like in their unique conglomeration of kaleidoscopes." Over time, through check-ins, lab investigations, and notebook projects, students build relationships, and also offer "unique perspectives on safe spaces on campus, micro-communities, local engagement opportunities and social prescriptions [to each other]—information I do not often have access to as someone increasingly distant from the real-time culture of undergraduate student life on campus," currie writes. This arrangement not only provides students with peer support but fundamentally challenges the assumption that instructors are, or should be, "the sole arbiters of meaningful classroom care."[20]

Facilitating the formation of such groups takes time and planning, but students in currie's courses report that the practice has a tremendous effect on their success. "Having a sense of community throughout ENGL 109 really changed the way I wrote. I felt like having that community that was supportive and wanted everyone to improve took away a lot of the stress that came out of writing and editing your own work," writes Jake. "It was pleasant to recognize how I was learning amongst others and because our strengths and weaknesses were different, we were able to help each other grow," writes Jasmine. "Feeling connected to your peers proved the writing experience to be more wholesome, pleasant, approachable, and because it helps remove a lot of the mental barriers of writing," writes Vivian, while Gabriel offers, "I was under the impression that I did not need classmates or teachers to help me succeed, which was my understanding of academic integrity at the time. I could not have been more wrong."[21]

There are historically a lot of reasons for students to resist the idea of group work. Often instructors ask groups to work outside of class without considering that students often have conflicting schedules, especially if they have jobs or care responsibilities. We should not only think about these considerations but offer up in-class time for collaboration on a regular schedule. If we think we don't have time for this, we need to go back to the drawing board and consider whether our assessments and content are in proper balance and calibrate both. Where group work is graded, students can feel resentful toward one another because they have different levels of commitment toward earning "good" grades, while interpersonal conflict—Who will lead? Does one person always get relegated to taking all the notes?—can derail projects altogether. This is why group work needs structure if it is to go well: it requires mechanisms by which students learn to step up and step back from leadership, to self-assess, and to become invested in a definition of success that is more than individual. There are excellent resources offering sample frameworks for structuring such work online.[22]

Participating in Learning

If our task as instructors is to teach to the whole student, rejecting the banking model of education described by Freire, we must invite students to be collaborators in their learning. For many instructors this means, in part, some variation of class participation. What this looks like for each field varies greatly, as do the vehicles we use to make participation possible: surveys, Zoom chats, clicker polls, Jamboard, discussion sections, Q and A sessions, or hands-on learning with clay, violas, prairie grass, and fish bones.[23] Participatory learning makes concepts stick, creates a dynamic of collaboration in our classroom spaces, and disrupts the one-way dynamic of the "sage on the stage" to whom students are a nameless, voiceless mass.[24] Class participation is already pretty broadly understood to be vital—so much so that many educators offer (and deduct) points for those who volunteer their thoughts, problem sets, and artwork (or don't), and weave this into a student's course grade. Yet, what does it mean to participate *well*? And how do students learn the parameters of participation in our courses?

Participation can and should be taught. It is not enough to consider class participation to be a vehicle for the absorption of class content; it has to be a skill that we give students time to develop. As Brenna Clarke Gray writes, "If you evaluate for it, you have to teach it. That's the rule. Otherwise, your course becomes an opaque mess of a game of 'guess what's in the professor's head' and that's not actually learning."[25] Most educators have an ideal in mind when they think about what class participation should look like, but not everyone works backward from that ideal to ask themselves what they will do to bring it about. How will we make sure that everyone has an equal chance to participate? How will we facilitate conversation so that no one dominates or, alternately, is left behind? Have we considered the strengths of the students in front of us, the varied cultural and social backgrounds from which they draw their understanding of what their role in participation should be, and the challenges they may face in conceptualizing their thoughts, expressing their opinions, or communicating in the format we've selected? Have we thought critically about the power differential between an instructor and a student and how that might condition certain student responses in a classroom, be it online or off?

One way to begin this work is to establish a set of community rules for class participation that speaks directly to both the atmosphere of collaboration you want to encourage and the responsibility everyone shares to make it happen. Here, as in many other things, I am profoundly influenced by the Intergroup Dialogue work done at the University of Michigan. Dialogue circles establish community guidelines that structure all group conversations, and the ground rules I share with my classes are adapted from those I first encountered in 2013. In one rule, for example, we agree that while it's okay to talk about our learning with people outside our class, we won't associate names with anecdotes, so that people can trust that what they share in the classroom will not become the stuff of gossip. We commit to paying attention to the wisdom our emotions can offer, as well as the insights offered by our intellects, so that everyone feels their whole selves are welcome. We agree to challenge ideas, but not people—to ask for evidence of a claim, perhaps, or to ask a clarifying question, but not to call others names. We also promise to balance "stepping up and stepping back"—to be aware of how much space we are taking up in conversation and how much space we need to create for others to share their thoughts. Michigan offers further examples of community guidelines on a handout hosted at the Intergroup Relations website.[26]

For such guidelines to become true community documents, they require student input. I often bring a list of guidelines to class and ask students what they like, what seems fair, what seems unfair, and where we might edit language for greater clarity. Sometimes we add a rule to speak to a student concern that the guidelines don't already address. This process doesn't have to be done during class time; you can ask students to annotate a set of guidelines, the results of which you can compile to inform group edits. Given more time, you might have the class build the guidelines from scratch. Student suggestions for rules to include could come in writing or be shared verbally, and then a rough draft of a document could shared with everyone in order to facilitate a feedback loop. Whatever your method of including students in the process of establishing ground rules, be sure to finish up by asking students to affirm that they will be guided by the finished document throughout the duration of your class. Don't then set the guidelines aside and forget about them: Refer to them during the semester so that the rules have life. I will sometimes ask students to pull up the guidelines on their devices or refer to a paper copy that I hand out in class, and we will all select one element as an intention for class discussion that day. This emphasizes that community building is an ongoing project and gives us an opportunity to review where we're meeting class goals and where we need to put in some practice.

Just as there's no single way to invite students to collaborate in setting ground rules, there's no single method of class participation that is uniformly equitable. For many years I ran my classes based on discussion and graded students on how well they participated. This certainly made for a classroom where we built on each other's insights and crowd-sourced our learning, but it was impossible for students to navigate if they had social anxiety or needed time to formulate their thoughts before contributing. It was only after students came to me during drop-in hours to share that they were worried about their participation grade that I realized how much I had assumed about the readiness, willingness, and ability of students to enter into these conversations. I began to allow those students to write me emails at the end of a week, reflecting on what they'd learned, offering their perspective on the topics we'd covered, and asking questions. I then realized that doing this only for those students who sought me out was inequitable in and of itself, so I offered the same opportunity to everyone. Eventually, I flipped things around and asked students to complete a short, ungraded reading reflection before each class and got rid of participation grades altogether.[27]

The prevailing method of participation in your field may differ from mine. Writing workshops, studio art classes, musical performances, and math labs all have different modes in which students contribute ideas and receive feedback or critique. What's key is participation itself. Research shows that even in enormous lecture settings, for example, where discussion may not be feasible because of class size and classroom architecture, student participation is still vital if the learning we hope to facilitate is to occur.[28] My colleagues at Knox make great use of clickers to gather data from students (attendance, for example), reasoned guesses as to which of several answers is the correct outcome of an equation, and votes that prioritize how groups should organize the different elements of a complex project. While clickers represent a hardware investment on the part of an institution, there arc also apps that allow students to vote in polls on their phones. At Knox we use Mentimeter to vote during faculty meetings, and there are many similar apps, such as Poll Everywhere and Slido.[29] If you prefer low-tech options, bring small pieces of paper and pencils to class and ask for a volunteer to collect votes and tally them. When you don't need immediate feedback, share an online form to conduct an in-class survey. If you're teaching using Zoom or Webex or any other number of live streaming platforms, experiment with polling and encourage the use of the chat for conversation about the day's work. You can pose questions there, solicit feedback, and give students who don't want to speak out loud an opportunity to share their thoughts. In every instance, think hard about who—because of disability, fear, or even a troubled friendship with another student in class—feels confident collaborating in the mode upon which you've settled, and build in variation. We can do much to build our students' skills at contributing to discussion and processing feedback, but we should also make space for the fact that we need multiple points of entry into those activities if our classrooms are to be just.

Remember that when a discipline prioritizes one method of communication over others—writing over speaking; speaking over making; making over writing—we are narrowing our students' ability to not only express what they know but to learn new things altogether. To tackle this in my own classroom, I not only ask my students to write—freewrites, reflections, lists, discussion questions—but I will ask my students to draw. I am not assessing their artistic ability by doing so, but I am offering them the chance to retrieve information from their memories about class themes and daily readings, and express their understanding of those topics in new ways. We draw inelegant maps to turn written information into geographic knowledge; we render scholarly articles as front-page newspaper articles; we take census data and draw complicated family trees; we draw asset maps of ourselves and our skills.[30] We also go beyond two-dimensional projects. Together, we create timelines and discuss their limitations for showing cultural movements and thematic elements that stretch for decades, and then I have students build 3D expressions of time to have them think of solutions to this problem. Students have used fabric scraps, bubble wrap, model atoms from chemistry class, and dowel rods to figure out a spatial expression of time that permits a deeper wrangling with the issue of what we know about the past.[31] In offering students these opportunities to be creative, I am making space for different students to share different strengths and ceding the space of telling students information to allow them to discover things for themselves.

Difficult Conversations

I'm often asked how we can be kind during heated classroom conversations, when a student says something—accidentally or intentionally—oppressive or offensive toward others in the room. I know that before I taught (and for some time afterwards) this was one of my biggest fears. Would I handle things the right way? Would I make things worse? I clearly remember a first-year seminar that I led early in my career as a professor where the class was discussing issues related to gender. One student said that she thought of her gender as a fantastical creature, and another student burst into laughter. Horrified, I sent the second student out of the room and sternly reminded the rest of the students that in *this* classroom we respected people. But my own actions were not clearly about respect; they were about shock, and feeling awful for the student who had confessed something deeply personal, and wanting to make an illustrative example of the student who laughed. I was also afraid that I was a bad teacher—not just in that moment but for weeks afterward— because the conflict had happened at all.

It's common for us to fear the storm of emotions that unlooked-for comments can unleash. Our reactions—our wish to protect ourselves and others; our wish to avoid conflict; our wish to educate—are often at war with one another and can lead to us feeling frozen in place. Even today, when such moments arise in my classroom, I often feel my thinking grow slow and unfocused while my heart rate quickens. I become acutely aware of having the most power in the room and often feel like the situation is one I alone must solve. This is absolutely normal, if misguided, as are a hundred other ways of reacting when we feel surprised, threatened, or outraged. It can help a great deal to do groundwork ahead of time to prepare for such moments, giving us more choices when it comes to selecting our in-the-moment response.

Preparing for the unexpected may seem paradoxical: it's unlikely we can predict when or how we'll be caught off guard. But we can pave the way toward compassionate resolution of classroom tensions by applying our self-awareness and cultivating that ability in others. The social identity reflection that I shared in chapter one provides one way to help students develop a new kind of self-awareness—and to get to know one another—at the beginning of a course. I have students fill the sheet out on the first day—sometimes on a paper I provide, sometimes by copying a Google Doc I've made—and create their own individual list. I make it clear that I will not be reading the reflections, that they will never have to share anything they feel uncomfortable disclosing, and, crucially, that I will go first. I model how to complete the chart, demonstrating both that I believe in transparency and that their answers can be single words or whole paragraphs; there's no incorrect way to complete the task.

It's worth pausing to acknowledge that transparency about social identities can be tricky. While I feel comfortable sharing my responses to every category on the list with my students, that will not be true for everyone in every situation. There are good reasons not to share certain parts of ourselves, especially when we lack power. If you're a graduate student, a contingent faculty member, or someone whose membership in certain social groups means you are constantly fighting against discrimination, you do not have a responsibility to put yourself in, at best, an awkward position and, at worst, one that could present real danger to your person or livelihood. If that is your situation, pick the categories you feel you can share ahead of time. Pick something to which you can offer a one-word answer and something that requires a little more explanation in order to model that there's no wrong way to respond to the questions. Leave it at that. Just as students need not share anything from their list that they want to keep private, the same is true for educators.

After students fill out the chart, I pair people up and ask them to have a conversation about the process of reflecting on identity. This is a moment to reiterate that they do not need to disclose each of their answers in order to participate but instead can have a more abstract conversation about why I assigned the task if they prefer. When we reconvene as a whole group, I ask the same questions about privilege and oppression as I was asked the first time that I undertook the exercise. This makes for a strong segue into talking about times when we might feel strong emotional responses to class material or conversations and how those moments connect to the very core of who we are. I share that when we feel a strong emotional response to a reading, an exercise, or a discussion, it is likely that one or more of our social identities has taken a hit. It can help us enormously to navigate tense moments if we know where and why we're feeling as we are.

I invite students to consider strong emotional reactions even more directly in a subsequent class period, utilizing resources from the Michigan Program on Intergroup Relations.[32] Individually and then together, we identify the ways in which we usually react when feeling big emotions in a classroom setting: we might go silent, rationalize the situation, leave the room, blurt out our feelings, laugh, or numb ourselves to our surroundings, for example. We then consider a range of common scenarios—someone interrupts us, says something offensive, derails the conversation, or tries to bully someone—and estimate how large an emotional reaction we would have if it happened to or around us. Finally, we work individually on a handout that asks us to remember a time when we had a strong emotional reaction in class, how we handled it, and how we would like to handle a similar reaction in the future. Robert R. Stains Jr. and John Sarrouf call this sort of work "reflection, preparation, prediction and rehearsal . . . leaving people better-resourced and more able to speak from the heart."[33]

The goal of all of this work is to enable resolution when things go awry. After thinking about our emotional reactions in the abstract, we are better positioned to name our feelings and consider the options for how we might respond when an unexpected event occurs in class. Rehearsing our optimum response to a situation is not a means of circumventing emotions, and it will not guarantee that we will always get things right, but it does mean that we have a catalog of possible responses in our brains from which we might choose when things are difficult. This is much easier than trying to generate a flawless approach in a moment of great stress. "I think oftentimes [in such situations], it can be seductive to want to shame or embarrass the person for what they've said, or what they've done, but where's the learning in that?" suggests Intergroup Dialogue expert Roger Fisher."[34] Pausing is an and invaluable and underappreciated pedagogical skill. Taking a breath and naming the action—"Hold on. We need to pause for a second"—does not dismiss anyone, shame anyone, or demand that anyone put aside their feelings. It does, however, signal that we can be thoughtful even as our emotions churn.

With a pause under our belts, we can respond. One way in which I have learned to process emotional moments in class is to name what's happened and ask questions that make space for further conversation: "I'm feeling frustrated right now. Does anyone else feel the same way?" As Dialogue facilitator Shaima Abdullah puts it, this approach isn't "me trying to attack [a student] by naming a certain behavior or a certain word that they had said, but actually an opportunity of me trying to invest in them ... I can see the possibility for change in you. ... So [I am] reminding them that this is something mutual that's happening and not something I am correcting. I'm not correcting a behavior for you. I am here trying to let you know how I'm feeling about this, and how the rest of the group is feeling about this."[35] I've also learned that asking a clarifying question can defuse a great deal of tension. Questions like "Where did you first learn that?" divert the conversation away from the oppositional and defensive thinking that we can all fall into in moments of stress.

If a student's comment or question is so offensive, so personal, or so destabilizing that you feel you cannot continue with class, extend that initial pause, name the situation ("This situation needs our time and reflection. We'll return to it in our next class."), and let the class go. This is not the end of the matter. First, seek out care for yourself. Talk to a trusted colleague, call a friend, engage with a mental health professional—reach out to whoever will help you process the situation and tend to your emotional needs. Is the situation one that needs attention from someone of a higher rank? Consider if you should call in your chair or dean, or alert student development about the situation. Then reach out to your students and provide them with the opportunity to process their thoughts and feelings. This does not mean that you act as their counselor. Instead, you might provide a reflective prompt and ask them to record their reactions, either for themselves or to share with you. Consider how you would like to open the next class, and make space to begin the work of collective repair. As you mull over how you would like things to begin, consider the work being done on restorative justice, as well as other advice related to regaining momentum after a serious breach of trust.[36]

Repair work is not just for students. There will be times when we bungle our response, say something harmful (whether intended or otherwise), or cause hurt. In thinking about how to respond to those moments, I have been deeply influenced by the work of Rabbi Danya Ruttenberg. "We all cause harm sometimes," she writes in her book *On Repentance and Repair*:

> Maybe it's intentional, a result of a calculated attempt to gain power, or from a place of anger or spite. Maybe it's out of carelessness, or ignorance, a reaction to fear, or because we were overwhelmed and dropped some balls. Maybe it's because we were acting out of our own broken places or trauma, or because, in our attempt to protect some interests, we ran roughshod over others. Maybe it's because our smaller role in a larger system puts us in the position of perpetuating hurt or injustice.[37]

When we cause harm, we must make sure that there are community supports in place to help our students process and recover from that harm; we cannot demand that they come to us for that help. A colleague may be able to assist, or your chair, and there are a host of student services, including counseling, that you or others can remind your students are available to them. Then comes the work of mending what is broken. Ruttenberg suggests that there are four steps through which we should pass after causing harm: we must name what we did, commit to (and begin to) change, offer redress and accept the consequences of our actions, and make an apology. These steps, which draw on the work of twelfth-century Jewish scholar Maimonides, come from Jewish tradition but do not require connection to that tradition or belief in any higher power.[38] It is important to note that forgiveness on the part of those harmed is not a given in this scenario. Instead, we take responsibility for the thing we did wrong and work to prevent it from happening again because it is the right thing to do, an action that is vital to both the development of the self and our responsibility toward our community.

Harm prevention is a critical responsibility for educators. Another example of this work is to provide content warnings to our students. Despite the ongoing insistence of many educators that this is still a matter of debate, it is, without question, unkind to withhold the means by which students can navigate triggering content.[39] At issue is the question of trauma. Individuals who have been traumatized (by violence or assault, for example) may find themselves triggered when forced to relive those experiences through readings, films, discussions, and lectures (as well as other educational experiences, like role-play). When a person is triggered, they are often thrown back into the emotional and physical state they were in when originally traumatized. They can feel terror, disabling panic, very real physical pain, and profound spatial and temporal disorientation.[40] But if an individual knows that there are potentially traumatizing materials or experiences ahead, they can prepare for them. They can deploy coping mechanisms. A student may ask for page numbers where they'll find descriptions of graphic violence, sexual assault, or other traumatizing material, so that they can skip them while still reading the rest of their assigned text. They may ask for permission to step out of the classroom during a discussion or depiction of traumatic material. Many other coping skills are highly individualized; let students tell you what will help them.

Content warnings are about equity. If a student has PTSD from a traumatic experience, they have a disability that requires your attention like any other. But not every student who has been traumatized has PTSD or has a formal diagnosis. Therapy and psychiatric services are expensive and inequitably distributed, which can make getting a diagnosis difficult, and PTSD is only one outcome of being traumatized.[41] This is where the principles of UDL are once again of enormous help. There are experiences that people commonly find traumatizing, like graphic violence or sexual assault. We can warn for those things. We can also ask students to let us know if they need a warning for other situations or experiences. Here's the language I use on my syllabi: "I have tried to anticipate where you may need a content warning, but if you have concerns or want to check that a particular trigger has been taken into account, please let me know. I am happy to provide that warning so that you can interact with class material safely, and on your own terms."

Nothing replaces listening to students when they tell us what they need. A student may, for example, be able to deal with a generalized discussion of rape but not a graphic description of a rape occurring, or a generalized discussion of lynching as a tool of white supremacy but not a graphic photograph of someone being lynched. This is not about enabling student avoidance but rather about supplying students with the information and tools they need to engage in their education. Listening to students about ways to navigate triggering situations is not just good UDL practice but actively returns something to students—choice—that a traumatic experience often takes away.[42]

Kindness has a lot to do with accountability. It's not about being nice and creating a frictionless existence where we shield ourselves from critique. It requires inquiry, humility, and a sense of ourselves as people committed to ongoing learning and change. It looks outward to the ways in which we treat others, and it also urges us to look inward and practice care toward ourselves. It is a kindness to discover, develop, and sustain support networks, to find spaces in which we are heard, and to take time away from our institutions and the claims of the classroom. It is kindness to engage in mutual aid that can offer us strong support and groundedness, whether that support is from a colleague down the hall, across campus, or online. Kindness is also about outward-looking and inward-facing respect. It is not about "letting go" of how we feel or, on the other hand, developing an avoidant and obnoxious ego but instead about claiming space as ours because of our humanity, generosity, and expertise.

The biggest obstacle to kindness in the classroom is fear—and the antidote is self-knowledge. If we understand our teaching anxieties, we can meet ourselves with compassion, holding ourselves accountable, committing to further exploration of our positionality, and extending ourselves grace as appropriate. It's from that place, rooted in knowing what makes us tick (and resist and grow and change), that we can each extend kindness to others. Just as we must know our content before teaching it to others, we must know kindness in order to share it, sketching out its boundaries through our words and actions, accepting our clumsiest moments along with our most elegant. Without self-knowledge, without critical curiosity, without exploration of why we show up as we do in a classroom, we cannot build teaching lives on anything but sand. We deserve to launch into teaching each semester, each week, each day, from a solid foundation. Our students deserve teachers who are rooted, and growing, and kind.

CONCLUSION

We deserve an academy that is kind.

Somewhere along the way, many of us were taught that the academy should be a place of intense competition, where we had rivals, not colleagues; where the most important insights and best ideas were those that rose to the top by any means necessary; where our emotional lives were not just unwelcome but entirely unnecessary distractions from the Work. Our mentors taught a distressingly large number of us that students should be the last consideration on our list of things to care about; that they were coddled and unserious; and that they were out to scam their way to a degree. These suppositions were reinscribed upon us by the delegation of teaching responsibilities to untenured faculty and graduate students, who often found themselves badly supported (if at all) by our institutions; by research and administrative responsibilities that ate up time; and by promotion and review processes that failed to reward the hard work of teaching well. Getting a job and holding on to a job under oppressive conditions shattered so many of us.

There are dozens of words that could be used to describe this particular expression of higher ed, but none of them have compassion at their core. Higher education needs to get kind—aggressively kind; determinedly kind. We have had our fill of niceness; we have suffered beneath the weight of just "getting along." We need to shift every part of what we do to prioritize care and compassion, not only for our students but for ourselves. We deserve nothing short of transformation—a system of higher education in which we are each valued for the totality of who we are instead of only the products (books, bell curves, patents, performances) we are urged to create.

When I was an undergraduate student, navigating the hidden curriculum of my university with almost no money and with my sense of belonging under siege, I took a course on the Cold War. I knew next to nothing about U.S. politics or modern American history when I began, and felt mentally flung about in the class, as though I were in a small boat on rough seas. At some point, we were assigned Robert F. Kennedy's Day of Affirmation speech to read, an address given at the University of Cape Town, South Africa, in 1966. I didn't expect much from the reading—another Kennedy holding court did not interest me—but then I stumbled over these words: "Each time a man stands up for an ideal, or acts to improve the lot of others, or strikes out against injustice, he sends forth a tiny ripple of hope, and crossing each other from a million different centers of energy and daring those ripples build a current which can sweep down the mightiest walls of oppression and resistance."[1]

I felt like a struck bell. Instead of a single person doing singular things to try and stay afloat in an academic space where I felt unwelcome, I felt a sudden sense of *hope*. Was it possible I was part of something bigger than myself? I had no idea what I wanted to do with my life, but the idea that my actions—small, clumsy, and unsteady as they were—could join with those of others to add up to something significant . . . that was an incredible idea, a life vest thrown to me when I felt raw and uncertain.

This book is for everyone who feels tossed around in a small boat. Kindness matters. There are enormous problems in our places of work, and it will take sustained, collective action to wrest change from the seductive pull of inertia. Our students are traumatized, currently navigating college in a global pandemic, responding to the continuous brutalization of BIPOC bodies and minds by a white supremacist culture, looking for safety from a world that treats their gender and sexual identities as mere whims, and wrestling with ableism. We—the faculty and staff who collaborate with those students—experience these things too. The work ahead is to create a just and equitable world, and we are not powerless. The choices we make, minute by minute, day by day, make a difference. We need a compassion that is self-reflective, accountable, and generous to create spaces in which we might thrive.

We need to start with ourselves, practicing a kindness that might be sorely lacking in our work worlds otherwise. We need strong boundaries to which we will firmly hold, respect for our bodies' needs—food, rest, water, play—and connection to communities that can sustain and enliven us. We need to find community when we feel isolated and found communities where we feel grounded; we need to consider the work we do as collaborative and think about the mutual benefits that all of us—faculty, staff, and students—accrue when we prioritize care. It all begins with one choice, with one syllabus statement about email hours, with one calendar block closed off for lunch, with one message to someone with whom we feel a possible connection. And it takes practice, and stumbling, and recovery: these things are part of the process, not an indication that the process isn't worthwhile.

From the place within us that flourishes when we are kind to ourselves, we can reach out to be kind in our instruction. We need to start that work before we ever see a student's face on a Zoom call or in a physical classroom packed with desks. We need to design our syllabi to offer a welcome, to demonstrate that our students are seen in all their complexity, potential, and grace. We need breathing space built into the schema of our courses; we need time to teach the languages in which we are already fluent to those who are not; we need to remember to share the many skills that undergird the achievements we want students to make. We need to offer our syllabi as maps to those who are lost, and collaborate with students to make those documents come alive.

We should meet students with infectious curiosity, learning their names and their hopes and their needs. We must extend a welcome in the way we introduce ourselves and the methods we choose to have students introduce themselves to one another. We can work together, from the very start, to build community standards for debate, discussion, and critique that prioritize collaboration and have compassion at their core. We must anticipate student bewilderment, nervousness, enthusiasm, and joy, and work to meet even the most skeptical students, for whom academia has so far not been kind, with trust. We must remember that our students experience loss, and laptops genuinely do crash, and there can be a glitch in the learning management system, and people get sick. From day one, we can commit to a spaciousness that makes room for all of this and more.

Our classrooms—online and off—should be spaces of exploration. We must design for the broadest possible definition of accessibility, knowing that fulfilling accommodations is only the first step. We can make space for our physicists to draw, our artists to write, our writers to make things with their hands. We must gather student thoughts and ideas through assessments that provide choice and flexibility and that meet their questions with the means to solve for a dozen values of x. We must think of ourselves as tearing down obstacles, not putting them in students' way, and succeeding when they succeed, and not when they fail.

Kindness is a discipline. We need kindness when we are tired, discouraged, and overwhelmed, and our students do too. We may not feel a wellspring of compassion every day, in every moment, but we can act with kindness—*do* kindness—even when feeling depleted and withdrawn. Indeed, this may be when kindness is our most useful watchword; when we can default to the kind thing, the just thing, the equitable thing, despite feeling scared or exhausted. There is no downside to acting with compassion; there is much we are left to regret when we choose to be unkind. And kindness is the gentle voice that says, *Put down the pen, turn off the computer, leave the campus, go home; take the time you need—the space of a breath; the distance of a commute; the stretch of a weekend—to fill your own reserves.*

Kindness begins with one action. That action is different for everyone—every educator, every student—and I cannot tell you where you should begin. But remember that a tweak is better than stagnation; that we are called to change almost every minute of our lives, and we can choose the direction in which that will go. Start small, experiment, make mistakes, make revisions. Push back against the idea that students are our antagonists and that anyone should accept judgment, meanness, and disengagement as their due. We are messy and overworked; we laugh; we despair; we have a dozen to-do lists on our minds. Given all of this, we owe ourselves a generous, thoughtful answer to the question:

Why not be kind?

NOTES

Introduction

1. "Statement on Standards of Professional Conduct (Updated 2023)," American Historical Association, https://www.historians.org/jobs-and-professional-development/statements-standards-and-guidelines-of-the-discipline/statement-on-standards-of-professional-conduct. See also Deborah J. Cohan, "Professors Should Uphold Rigor When Assessing Students, Even in a Pandemic," Inside Higher Ed, August 24, 2021, https://www.insidehighered.com/advice/2021/08/25/professors-should-uphold-rigor-when-assessing-students-even-pandemic-opinion.

2. bell hooks, *Teaching to Transgress: Education as the Practice of Freedom* (New York: Routledge, 1994), 43.

3. It has been well established that women and genderqueer people of all races, as well as BIPOC men, are rated lower in student evaluations of teaching than their white male colleagues and often face discrimination in contract reviews. See, for example, Lillian MacNell, Adam Driscoll, and Andrea N. Hunt, "What's in a Name: Exposing Gender Bias in Student Ratings of Teaching," *Innovative Higher Education* 40 (2015): 291–303, https://doi.org/10.1007/s10755-014-9313-4; Anne Boring and Arnaud Philippe, "Reducing Discrimination in the Field: Evidence from an Awareness-Raising Intervention Targeting Gender Biases in Student Evaluations of Teaching," *Journal of Public Economics* 193 (January 2021): 104323, https://doi.org/10.1016/j.jpubeco.2020.104323; Jean Swindle and Larissa Malone, "Testimonials of Exodus: Self-Emancipation in Higher Education through the Power of Womanism," in *We're Not OK: Black Faculty Experiences and Higher Education Strategies*, ed. Antija M. Allen and Justin T. Stewart (Cambridge: Cambridge University Press, 2022), 147–68; and Armon R. Perry et al., "Understanding Student Evaluations: A Black Faculty Perspective," *Reflections: Narratives of Professional Helping* 20, no. 1 (November 2015): 29–35.

4. The University of Iowa School of Education conducted continuous evaluations of the Bringing History Home project, all of which are available at http://www.bringinghistoryhome.org/evaluations.

5. SOCC sheets adapted from the BHH model are available on my website: https://catherinedenial.org/blog/uncategorized/socc-it-primary-source-analysis-with-my-students/.

6. Intergroup Dialogue is, in the words of Ximena Zúñiga, "a face-to-face facilitated conversation between members of two or more social identity groups that strives to create new levels of understanding, relating, and action. The term social identity group refers to group affiliation based on a common status or history in society resulting from socially constructed group distinctions." "Bridging Differences through Dialogue," *About Campus* 7, no. 6 (January–February 2003): 9, https://doi.org/10.1177/108648220300700603.

7. For more on these issues, see Staci K. Haines, *The Politics of Trauma: Somatics, Healing, and Social Justice* (Berkeley, CA: North Atlantic Books, 2019); Devon Price, *Umasking Autism: Discovering the New Faces of Neurodiversity* (New York: Harmony, 2022); Leah Lakshmi Piepzna-Samarasinha, *Care Work: Dreaming Disability Justice* (Vancouver: Arsenal Pulp Press, 2018); and Thomas J. Tobin and Kirsten T. Behling, *Reach Everyone, Teach Everyone: Universal Design for Learning in Higher Education* (Morgantown: West Virginia University Press, 2018).

8. One of the central texts I read in this period that I still come back to again and again is Pema Chödrön's *When Things Fall Apart: Heart Advice for Difficult Times* (Boston: Shambala, 2000). The Dalai Lama of Tibet's books *My Land and My People: The Original Autobiography of His Holiness the Dalai Lama of Tibet* (New York: Warner Books, 1997) and *The Universe in a Single Atom: The Convergence of Science and Spirituality* (New York: Morgan Road Books, 2005) are also dog-eared and well thumbed. Other books that have been key to my shifting understanding of myself and kindness include Damien Keown's *Buddhism: A Very Short Introduction* (New York: Oxford University Press, 2013); Roger Kamenetz's *The Jew in the Lotus: A Poet's Rediscovery of Jewish Identity in Buddhist India* (New York: HarperOne, 2007); Mary Rose O'Reilley's *The Barn at the End of the World: The Apprenticeship of a Quaker, Buddhist Shepherd* (Minneapolis: Milkweed Editions, 2001); and Tara Brach's *Radical Acceptance: Embracing Your Life with the Heart of a Buddha* (New York: Random House, 2004).

9. Naomi Shihab Nye, "Kindness," 1995, Poets.org, https://poets.org/poem/kindness.

10. I explore this in more detail in chapter 2.

11. "Kyriarchy," as used in this way, was coined by Elizabeth Schüssler Fiorenza. For more on this definition, see, for example, Natalie Osborne, "Intersectionality and Kyriarchy: A Framework for Approaching Power and Social Justice in Planning and Climate Change Adaptation," *Planning Theory* 14, no. 2 (2015): 130–51, https://doi.org/10.1177/1473095213516443.

12. Some of the books that have been most instructional to me on this score include Piepzna-Samarasinha, *Care Work*; Waziyatawin, *What Does Justice Look Like? The Struggle for Liberation in Dakota Homeland* (St. Paul: Living Justice Press, 2008); Christina Sharpe, *In the Wake: On Blackness and Being* (Durham, NC: Duke University Press, 2016); Audre Lorde, *A Burst of Light and Other Essays* (1988; reprinted, New York: Ixia Press, 2017); Linda Tuhiwai Smith, *Decolonizing*

Methodologies: Research and Indigenous Peoples, 2nd ed. (London: Zed Books, 2012); Margaret Price, *Mad at School: Rhetorics of Mental Disability and Academic Life* (Ann Arbor: University of Michigan Press, 2014); and Bettina L. Love, *We Want to Do More Than Survive: Abolitionist Teaching and the Pursuit of Educational Freedom* (Boston: Beacon Press, 2019).

13. Kris MacDonald, "A Review of the Literature: The Needs of Non-Traditional Students in Post-Secondary Education," *Strategic Enrollment Management Quarterly* 5, no. 4 (January 2018): 159, 160, https://doi.org/10.1002/sem3 .20115; and "Nontraditional Undergraduates: Trends in Enrollment from 1986 to 1992 and Persistence and Attainment among 1989–90 Beginning Postsecondary Students," National Center for Education Statistics, Statistical Analysis Report, November 1996, https://nces.ed.gov/pubs/97578.pdf.

14. Lorelle L. Espinosa et al., "Enrollment in Undergraduate Education," in *Race and Ethnicity in Higher Education: A Status Report*, American Council on Education (2019): 37, 43, https://www.equityinhighered.org/wp-content /uploads/2019/02/Race-and-Ethnicity-in-Higher-Education.pdf.

15. *National College Health Assessment II: Undergraduate Student Reference Group, Executive Summary, Spring 2019*, American College Health Association, 2019, 17, https://www.acha.org/documents/ncha/NCHA-II_SPRING_2019 _UNDERGRADUATE_REFERENCE%20_GROUP_EXECUTIVE_SUMMARY .pdf.

16. "Students with Disabilities [2015–16]," National Center for Educational Statistics, accessed April 29, 2023, https://nces.ed.gov/fastfacts/display.asp ?id=60.

17. *The Hope Center Survey 2021: Basic Needs Insecurity in the Ongoing Pandemic*, Hope Center for College, Community, and Justice, March 31, 2021, 26, https:// hope.temple.edu/sites/hope/files/media/document/HopeSurveyReport2021.pdf.

18. Not every institution gathers every bit of this data, but Viji Sathy, Kelly A. Hogan, and Bob Henshaw suggest that it's possible to build a tool to help you understand your student body better: "The More You Know about Your Students, the More Inclusive You Can Be in the Classroom," *Chronicle of Higher Education*, June 21, 2022, https://www.chronicle.com/article/the-more-you-know-about -your-students-the-more-inclusive-you-can-be-in-the-classroom.

19. Here's a blog post I wrote before I went to the Digital Pedagogy Lab, about the preteaching jitters I used to get all the time: https://catherinedenial .org/blog/uncategorized/the-pre-teaching-jitters/.

20. Fall 2019 survey, Knox College, History 295-Z: History Pedagogy, in author's possession. Full copies of this survey are available on request.

Chapter 1. Kindness toward the Self

1. Yamiko Marama, "Reading Audre Lorde in the Age of #Self-Care," *Kill Your Darlings*, June 3, 2021, https://www.killyourdarlings.com.au/article

/rereading-audre-lorde-in-the-age-of-self-care/. A glance at *HuffPost*'s "self-care" tag is also instructive in this regard: https://www.huffpost.com/topic/self-care.

2. Googling "self-care" will bring up hundreds of articles and blog entries that use this framing. For example, Jamie Birt suggests that "by finding ways to replenish your well-being during work, you can be a more productive and motivated employee." "14 Ways to Practice Self-Care at Work (and Why It Matters)," *Indeed*, Updated August 31, 2023, https://www.indeed.com/career-advice/career-development/selfcare-at-work. The makers of the Calm app address business managers directly, suggesting, "Self-care alone won't solve burnout, but having it recognized as a priority within your organization can make a huge difference when it comes to building happier, more sustainable workday routines for you or your employees." "Creating a Culture of Self-Care in the Workplace," *Calm*, accessed April 29, 2023, https://business.calm.com/resources/blog/creating-a-culture-of-self-care-in-the-workplace. In "Six Ways to Weave Self-Care into Your Workday," Amy Jen Su suggests that while self-care should run through all aspects of our lives, it's ultimately about asking, *"Who and what can support and be in service of the positive contribution I hope to make?"* at work (italics in the original). *Harvard Business Review*, June 19, 2017, https://hbr.org/2017/06/6-ways-to-weave-self-care-into-your-workday.

3. Nel Noddings, *Caring: A Relational Approach to Ethics and Moral Education*, 2nd ed., updated (Berkeley: University of California Press, 2013), 24. It is, admittedly, not always easy to view ourselves with affection and regard. In those instances, it's useful to borrow someone else for a while—to ask ourselves how we would treat a treasured friend or family member in our situation and act accordingly.

4. "Background Facts on Contingent Faculty Positions," American Association of University Professors, accessed April 29, 2023, https://www.aaup.org/issues/contingency/background-facts; and Kaye Whitehead, Ariella Rotramel, Angela Clark-Taylor, and Heidi R. Lewis, "NWSA Statement on Threats to the Field in Higher Education and Beyond," National Women's Studies Association, accessed April 29, 2023, https://mailchi.mp/nwsa/nwsa-statement-on-threats-to-the-field-in-higher-education-and-beyond. For attacks upon teaching race in higher education, see the assembled links at the American Studies Association website, accessed April 29, 2023, https://www.theasa.net/about/news-events/announcements/resolution-defending-academic-freedom-against-attacks-%E2%80%9Ccritical-race. For information on patterns of sexual assault on US campuses, see "Campus Sexual Assault and Campus Climate," American Psychological Association, updated July 2019, https://www.apa.org/advocacy/interpersonal-violence/sexual-assault-campus-climate.pdf. For one example of how a campus has engaged with issues of sexual harassment, see Anemona Hartocollis, "A Lawsuit Accuses Harvard of Ignoring Sexual Harassment by a Professor," *New York Times*, February 8, 2022, https://www.nytimes.com/2022/02/08/us/harvard-sexual-harassment-lawsuit.html.

5. See, for example, Chrystal A. George Mwangi et al., "'Black Elephant in the Room': Black Students Contextualizing Campus Racial Climate within U.S. Racial Climate," *Journal of College Student Development* 59, no. 4 (July–August 2018): 456–74, https://doi.org/10.1353/csd.2018.0042; A. Skylar Joseph, "The Modern Trail of Tears: The Missing and Murdered Indigenous Women (MMIW) Crisis in the U.S.," *Journal of Forensic and Legal Medicine* 79 (April 2021): 102136, https://doi.org/10.1016/j.jflm.2021.102136; "'They Treat You Like You Are Worthless': Internal DHS Reports of Abuses by U.S. Border Officials," Human Rights Watch, October 21, 2021, https://www.hrw.org/report/2021/10/21/they-treat-you-you-are-worthless/internal-dhs-reports-abuses-us-border-officials#; Joe Hernandez, "1 in 4 American Jews Say They Experienced Anti-Semitism in the Last Year," NPR, October 26, 2021, https://www.npr.org/2021/10/26/1049288223/1-in-4-american-jews-say-they-experienced-antisemitism-in-the-last-year; and "Anti-Muslim Hatred Has Reached 'Epidemic Proportions,' Says UN Rights Expert, Urging Action by States," United Nations, March 4, 2021, https://news.un.org/en/story/2021/03/1086452.

6. As Alex Shevrin Venet puts it in *Equity-Centered Trauma-Informed Education* (New York: W. W. Norton, 2021), 10: "In learning more about trauma, it has become clear to me that our current educational system is not set up with the needs of trauma survivors in mind. Worse, school systems and individual educators can be the *perpetrators* of trauma."

7. Jina B. King and Sami Schalk, "Reclaiming the Radical Politics of Self-Care: A Crip-of-Color Critique," *South Atlantic Quarterly* 120, no. 2 (April 2021): 326, 327, https://doi.org/10.1215/00382876-8916074.

8. Marama, "Reading Audre Lorde," 199.

9. Travis Chi Wing Lau, "Slowness, Disability, and Academic Productivity," in Christopher McMaster and Benjamin Whitburn, eds., *Disability and the University: A Disabled Students' Manifesto* (New York: Peter Lang, 2019), 11–19.

10. Cate Denial, Clarissa Sorensen-Unruh, and Elizabeth Lehfeldt, "After the Great Pivot Should Come the Great Pause," *Chronicle of Higher Education*, February 25, 2022, https://www.chronicle.com/article/after-the-great-pivot-should-come-the-great-pause.

11. Catherine Denial and Gabrielle Raley-Karlin, "Ground Rules for Dialogue," adapted from "Ground Rules" from the Program on Intergroup Relations at the University of Michigan. Copies available from the author upon request.

12. Oliver Burkeman, *Four Thousand Weeks: Time Management for Mortals* (New York: Farrar, Straus and Giroux, 2021), 72–73.

13. For a sampling of these different perspectives, see Terrell E. Robinson and Warren C. Hope, "Teaching in Higher Education: Is There a Need for Training in Pedagogy in Graduate Degree Programs?," *Research in Higher Education Journal* 21 (August 2013), https://files.eric.ed.gov/fulltext/EJ1064657.pdf; James P. McCoy and Martin I. Milkman, "Do Recent PhD Economists Feel Prepared to Teach Economics?," *Journal of Economic Education* 41, no. 2 (April–June

2010): 211–15, https://www.jstor.org/stable/25766054; Nicola Justice, "Preparing Graduate Students to Teach Statistics: A Review of Research and Ten Practical Recommendations," *Journal of Statistics Education* 28, no. 3 (2020): 334–43, https://doi.org/10.1080/10691898.2020.1841590; and Jennifer Meta Robinson et al., "The Graduate Course in Pedagogy: Survey of Instructors of College Pedagogy in the United States and Canada," *College Teaching* 67, no. 2 (2019): 109–19, https://doi.org/10.1080/87567555.2018.1558171.

14. Derek Bruff, "In Defense of Continuous Exposition by the Teacher," *Agile Learning* (blog), September 15, 2015, https://derekbruff.org/?p=3126; Joshua R. Eyler, "The Inauthenticity of the Lecture," in *How Humans Learn: The Science and Stories Behind Effective College Teaching* (Morgantown: West Virginia University Press, 2018), 164–68; Scott Freeman et al., "Active Learning Increases Student Performance in Science, Engineering, and Mathematics," *Psychological and Cognitive Sciences* 111, no. 23 (May 2014): 8410–15, https://doi.org/10.1073/pnas.1319030111; and Thomas Buchanan and Edward Palmer, "Student Perceptions of the History Lecture: Does This Delivery Mode Have a Future in the Humanities?," *Journal of University Learning & Teaching Practice* 14, no. 2 (2017), https://doi.org/10.53761/1.14.2.4. For a defense of the lecture, see Molly Worthen, "Lecture Me. Really," *New York Times*, October 17, 2015, https://www.nytimes.com/2015/10/18/opinion/sunday/lecture-me-really.html.

15. See Cate Denial @cjdenial, Twitter, February 3, 2020, https://twitter.com/cjdenial/status/1224371940649054210.

16. For a multifaceted discussion of this point, see Jessamyn Neuhaus, ed., *Picture a Professor: Interrupting Biases about Faculty and Increasing Student Learning* (Morgantown: West Virginia University Press, 2022.)

17. This understanding of our collective socialization as being the absorption of misinformation about ourselves and others comes, in part, from the sample Ground Rules for Dialogue at the University of Michigan's Program in Intergroup Relations. On this process regarding race in particular, see also Bettina L. Love, "White Teachers Need Anti-Racist Therapy," *Education Week*, February 6, 2020, https://www.edweek.org/ew/articles/2020/02/07/all-teachers-need-therapy-white-teachers-need.html.

18. Jesica Siham Fernández, "Critical Reflexivity as a Tool for Students: A First Day of Class Conversation on What a Professor Looks Like," in Neuhaus, ed., *Picture a Professor*, 59. See also Henrika McCoy, "What Do You Call a Black Woman with a PhD? A N*****: How Race Trumps Education No Matter What," *Race and Justice* 11, no. 3 (July 2021): 318–27, https://doi.org/10.1177/2153368720988892; and Kerry Ann Rockquemore, "Call Me Doctor ____," *Inside Higher Ed*, March 11, 2015, https://www.insidehighered.com/advice/2015/03/11/advice-young-black-woman-academe-about-not-being-called-doctor.

19. See, for example, Lillian MacNell, Adam Driscoll, and Andrea N. Hunt, "What's in a Name? Exposing Gender Bias in Student Ratings of Teaching," *Innovative Higher Education* 40 (2015): 291–303, https://doi.org/10.1007/s10755

-014-9313-4; and Anne Boring and Arnaud Philippe, "Reducing Discrimination in the Field: Evidence from an Awareness-Raising Intervention Targeting Gender Biases in Student Evaluations of Teaching," *Journal of Public Economics* 193 (January 2021): 104323, https://doi.org/10.1016/j.jpubeco.2020.104323.

20. "Social Identity Wheel," LSA Inclusive Teaching, University of Michigan, accessed April 29, 2023, https://sites.lsa.umich.edu/inclusive-teaching /social-identity-wheel/.

21. This is not exclusively the case. As we learn more about our privileges, hopefully we develop an awareness of them in action and think about them often.

22. adrienne maree brown, *Emergent Strategy: Shaping Change, Changing Worlds* (Chico, CA: AK Press, 2017), 52–53.

23. "We are rewarded for curiosity by dopamine and opioids (feel-good chemicals in the brain), which are stimulated in the face of something new. Because our brains evolved to remain vigilant to a constantly changing environment, we learn better in brief intervals. This is likely one reason why variation in materials, breaks, and even intermittent naps facilitate learning," writes Louis Cozolino, "Nine Things Educators Need to Know about the Brain," Greater Good Magazine, March 19, 2013, https://greatergood.berkeley.edu/article/item /%20nine_things_educators_need_to_know_about_the_brain.

24. As James Oppenheim wrote in his poem "Bread and Roses" in 1911, "Our lives shall not be sweated from birth until life closes; / Hearts starve as well as bodies; give us bread, but give us roses." "Bread and Roses," Zinn Education Project, reprinted from Labor Notes 2007, https://www.zinnedproject.org /materials/bread-and-roses-song/.

25. This was a situation that received particular attention during the COVID-19 pandemic. See, for example, Jennifer Liu, "When Work and Home Are the Same Place, Experts Say This Is How to Find Balance," CNBC, March 27, 2020, https://www.cnbc.com/2020/03/27/when-work-and-home-are-the-same -place-this-is-how-to-find-balance.html; John Herrman, "The Buy-Nothing Home Office," *New York Times*, April 15, 2020, https://www.nytimes.com/2020/04/15 /style/working-from-home-setup.html; and Danielle Abril, "Ask Help Desk: How Remote Workers Can Separate Home and Work Lives," *Washington Post*, October 29, 2021, https://www.washingtonpost.com/technology/2021/10/29/ask-help -desk-remote-work-return-to-office-tablets-laptops/.

26. Anne Helen Petersen, "The Case for Lunch," *Culture Study* (blog), June 19, 2022, https://annehelen.substack.com/p/the-case-for-lunch.

27. Catherine Denial, "Burning Out and Firing Up," *Cate Denial* (blog), July 12, 2019, https://catherinedenial.org/blog/uncategorized/burning-out-and -firing-up/; and Beth Godbee, "Beth Godbee, Ph.D.," Head-Heart-Hands.com, July 12, 2019, https://heart-head-hands.com/beth-godbee/.

28. René Brooks, "How to Guard Your Yes (and Figure Out When You Haven't Been Doing It!)," *Black Girl, Lost Keys* (blog), April 13, 2020, https:// blackgirllostkeys.com/adhd/how-to-guard-your-yes/.

29. James Hollis, *What Matters Most: Living a More Considered Life* (New York: Gotham Books, 2009), 71.

30. Did you know that Monopoly was, in its original form, created with two sets of rules, one that allowed all money to be distributed equally, and one that did not? Eula Bliss, "The Landlord's Game: Eula Bliss on the Anticapitalist Origins of Monopoly," Literary Hub, September 2, 2020, https://lithub.com/the -landlords-game-eula-biss-on-the-anticapitalist-origins-of-monopoly/.

31. "Humans are inherently social. We are not special in this way; it is hard to think of any animal for whom the regulation of social behaviour is not important." Simon N. Young, "The Neurobiology of Human Social Behaviour: An Important but Neglected Topic," *Journal of Psychiatry and Neuroscience* 33, no. 5 (2008): 391. See also Michael Tomasello, "The Ultra-Social Animal," *European Journal of Social Psychology* 44, no. 3 (April 2014): 187–94, https://doi.org /10.1002/ejsp.2015.

32. For a good overview of this topic, see Mark Bowers et al., *Solitary Confinement as Torture.* University of North Carolina School of Law Immigration/ Human Rights Clinic, 2014, 145–65, https://law.unc.edu/wp-content/uploads /2019/10/solitaryconfinementreport.pdf.

33. Karin Brulliard, "Social Distancing Is So Hard because It's Contrary to Human Nature," *Washington Post*, March 17, 2020, https://www.washington post.com/science/2020/03/17/coronavirus-social-distancing/; and Greg Miller, "Social Distancing Prevents Infections, but It Can Have Unintended Consequences," *Science*, March 16, 2020, https://www.science.org/content/article/we -are-social-species-how-will-social-distancing-affect-us.

34. Em Win, "How to Host a Restorative Dinner Party for Your Chosen Queer Fam," Autostraddle, June 14, 2022, https://www.autostraddle.com/how-to -host-a-restorative-dinner-party-for-your-chosen-queer-fam/?utm_source=pocket _mylist.

35. For a thoughtful discussion of the costs of being on social media, as well as suggestions for ways to make social media a more welcoming and healthy space, see Kaitlin Curtice, "What Do We Do When Our Favorite Leaders Leave Social Media Behind?," *Liminality Journal* (blog), June 23, 2022, https:// kaitlincurtice.substack.com/p/what-do-we-do-when-our-favorite-leaders.

36. The University of Mary Washington's Domain of One's Own program has a series of modules you can work through to become a more savvy user of platforms, apps, and boards, to understand issues of privacy and security, and to think about what it means to be a good digital citizen: "Building Blocks for Domain of One's Own," University of Mary Washington, accessed April 29, 2023, https://umw.domains/modules/.

37. Allie Volpe, "Why Community Matters So Much—and How to Find Yours," Vox, March 24, 2022, https://www.vox.com/22992901/how-to-find-your -community-as-an-adult; VolunteerMatch, https://www.volunteermatch.org/; and Jenny Anderson, "The Only Metric of Success That Really Matters Is the One We

Ignore," Quartz, March 12, 2019, https://qz.com/1570179/how-to-make-friends
-build-a-community-and-create-the-life-you-want/.

38. Michelle A. Barton et al., "Stop Framing Wellness Programs around
Self-Care," *Harvard Business Review*, April 4, 2022, https://hbr.org/2022/04
/stop-framing-wellness-programs-around-self-care.

39. Sarah Rose Cavanagh, *The Spark of Learning: Energizing the College
Classroom with the Science of Emotion* (Morgantown: West Virginia University
Press, 2016), 24; and Mary Helen Immordino-Yang, *Emotions, Learning, and the
Brain: Exploring the Educational Implications of Affective Neuroscience* (New York:
W. W. Norton, 2016), 18.

40. Caring is socially scripted as "feminine" work, suggests Nora Samaran, and that script is deeply tied to misogyny. "We must call on masculinity to
become whole and nurturing of self and others, to recognize that attachment
needs are healthy and normal and not 'female,' and thus to expect of men to heal
themselves and others the same way we expect women to be nurturers," she
writes in *Turn the World Inside Out: The Emergence of Nurturance Culture* (Chico,
CA: AK Press, 2019), 19–20.

41. One example of these tropes in action can be found in Joseph M.
Keegin, "The Hysterical Style in the American Humanities: On the Ideological
Posturing and Moral Nitpicking of the Very Online," *Chronicle of Higher Education*, June 15, 2022, https://www.chronicle.com/article/the-hysterical-style-in-the
-american-humanities.

42. "Ohio 4-H Healthy Living Journal," Ohio State University, accessed
April 29, 2023, https://u.osu.edu/4hjournal/.

43. "Lifestyle Spending Account," Ohio State University, accessed April
29, 2023, https://hr.osu.edu/benefits/lsa/.

44. "New Wellness Benefits Available to Eligible Faculty and Staff," Ohio
State University, January 26, 2023, https://hr.osu.edu/news/2023/01/26/new
-wellness-benefits-available-for-eligible-faculty-and-staff/.

45. "United Way: Compassion Fund," University of Notre Dame, accessed
April 29, 2023, https://unitedway.nd.edu/compassion-fund/; "Graduate Student Emergency Support Fund," University of Notre Dame, Graduate School,
accessed April 29, 2023, https://graduateschool.nd.edu/policies-forms/graduate
-student-assistance/graduate-student-emergency-support-fund/. Notre Dame
also maintains food assistance for graduate students, but this is not a perk—it is
evidence of graduate stipends being far too low.

46. Karen Ray Costa, email to author, June 25, 2022. Copies available upon
request.

47. Dean Spade, *Mutual Aid: Building Solidarity during This Crisis (and the
Next)* (London, Verso Books, 2020), 7.

48. Alexandria Ocasio-Cortez and Mariame Kaba, "Mutual Aid 101 Toolkit," accessed April 29, 2023, https://cdn.cosmicjs.com/09a653b0-7545-11ea
-be6b-9f10a20c6f68-Mutual-Aid-101-Toolkit.pdf.

49. Costa, email to author, June 25, 2022. Credit also to my colleague Courtney Joseph for coining the phrase "lifeboat learning."

50. Spade, *Mutual Aid*, 9–20.

51. See, for example, Ezra Marcus, "How College Students Are Helping Each Other Survive," *New York Times*, November 23, 2020, https://www.nytimes.com /2020/11/23/style/college-mutual-aid-networks.html; Abdullah Shihipar, "These Students Took Care of Each Other When Their Universities Didn't," *Nation*, April 13, 2020, https://www.thenation.com/article/society/these-students-took -care-of-each-other-when-their-universities-didnt/; and Lucia Geng, "Mutual Aid Goes Mainstream," *Dissent*, Fall 2021, https://www.dissentmagazine.org/article /mutual-aid-goes-mainstream.

Chapter 2. Kindness and the Syllabus

1. Paulo Freire, *Pedagogy of the Oppressed*, 50th anniversary ed. (New York: Bloomsbury, 2018), 72.

2. Donna Mejia, "The Superpowers of Visual Ambiguity: Transfiguring My Experience of Colorism and Multiheritage Identity for Educational Good," in Jessamyn Neuhaus, ed., *Picture a Professor: Interrupting Biases about Faculty and Increasing Student Learning* (Morgantown: West Virginia University Press, 2022), 247.

3. When Jesica Siham Fernández took her first psychology class with a Chicana feminist professor, "the encounter shattered my assumptions about the professoriate, and I realized that I could one day too be a professor!" See "Critical Reflexivity as a Tool for Students Learning to Recognize Biases," in Neuhaus, *Picture a Professor*, 53. See also Silvia Lorena Mazzula, "Wholeness and Hope in Education: This Is What a Professor Looks Like," *Psych Learning Curve*, May 7, 2018, http://psychlearningcurve.org/wholeness-and-hope-in-education-this-is-what-a -professor-looks-like/.

4. Christine M. Harrington and Crystal A. Gabert-Quillen's research into the best length for a syllabus found that students in their focus groups agreed that certain things should be in the document: "grading information, course outline, professor contact information, policy information, books and online materials needed, specific due dates, visual appeal (color, images, graphic art), course description, clear and organized information, and assignment details." Christine M. Harrington and Crystal A. Gabert-Quillen, "Syllabus Length and Use of Images: An Empirical Investigation of Student Perceptions," *Scholarship of Teaching and Learning in Psychology* 1, no. 3 (2015): 235–43, https://doi.org/10 .1037/stl0000040.

5. Harrington and Gabert-Quillen, "Syllabus Length," 1–2.

6. Kevin Gannon, "How to Create a Syllabus: Advice Guide," *Chronicle of Higher Education*, accessed May 1, 2023, https://www.chronicle.com/article/how -to-create-a-syllabus/.

7. You can find one version of my introductory video at https://learning incommon.org/.

8. Michelle Pacansky-Brock, "The Liquid Syllabus: An Anti-Racist Teaching Element," C2C Digital Magazine, Spring/Summer 2021, https://scalar.usc .edu/works/c2c-digital-magazine-spring--summer-2021/the-liquid-syllabus -anti-racist. Pacansky-Brock offers a public, online course titled "Creating a Liquid Syllabus" at https://ccconlineed.instructure.com/courses/6771, accessed May 1, 2023.

9. There are many theories as to why students cheat, among them the pressure to perform well academically, which can generate great anxiety. See Angela D. Miller, Tamera B. Murdock, and Morgan M. Grotewiel, "Addressing Academic Dishonesty among the Highest Achievers," *Theory into Practice* 56, no. 2 (2017): 121–28, https://doi.org/10.1080/00405841.2017.1283574; Kyle A. Burgason, Ophir Sefiha, and Lisa Briggs, "Cheating Is in the Eye of the Beholder," *Innovative Higher Education* 44 (June 2019): 203–19, https://doi.org/10.1007 /s10755-019-9457-3; and B. D. Jenkins et al., "When Opportunity Knocks: College Students' Cheating amid the COVID-19 Pandemic," *Teaching of Psychology* 50, no. 4 (2023): 407–19, https://doi.org/10.1177/00986283211059067.

10. A quick Google search will turn up the attendance policies for dozens of different campuses as well as a variety of student newspapers tackling this issue. For a sampling of perspectives on attendance, see Jo Ann M. Pinto and Peter Lohrey, "Point-Counterpoint: Should Attendance Be Required in Collegiate Classrooms?," *Contemporary Issues in Education Research* 9, no. 3 (2016): 115–19, https://doi.org/10.19030/cier.v9i3.9706; Kelli Marshall, "Why I Don't Take Attendance," *Chronicle of Higher Education*, October 12, 2017, https://www.chronicle .com/article/why-i-dont-take-attendance/; Stefan Bücele, "Evaluating the Link between Attendance and Performance in Higher Education: The Role of Classroom Engagement Dimensions," *Assessment and Evaluation in Higher Education* 46, no. 1 (2021): 132–50, https://doi.org/10.1080/02602938.2020.1754330.

11. Hilde de Ridder-Symoens, ed., *A History of the University in Europe*, Vol. 1, *Universities in the Middle Ages* (Cambridge: Cambridge University Press, 1992). For histories of American higher education, see Roger L. Geiger, *The History of American Higher Education: Learning and Culture from the Founding to World War II* (Princeton, NJ: Princeton University Press, 2016); John R. Thelin, *A History of American Higher Education*, 3rd ed. (Baltimore: Johns Hopkins University Press, 2019); Nathan M. Sorber, *Land-Grant Colleges and Popular Revolt: The Origins of the Morrill Act and the Reform of Higher Education* (Ithaca, NY: Cornell University Press, 2018); Craig Steven Wilder, *Ebony and Ivory: Race, Slavery , and the Troubled History of America's Universities* (New York: Bloomsbury, 2014); and T. Elon Dancy, II, Kirsten T. Edwards, and James Earl Davis, "Historically White Universities and Plantation Politics: Anti-Blackness and Higher Education in the Black Lives Matter Era," *Urban Education* 53, no. 2 (2018): 176–95, https://doi .org/10.1177/0042085918754328.

12. Sara Goldrick-Rab, "Basic Needs Security and the Syllabus," *Medium*, accessed May 1, 2023, August 7, 2017, https://saragoldrickrab.medium.com/basic -needs-security-and-the-syllabus-d24cc7afe8c9. The Open CoLab at Plymouth State University offers a variety of resources for instructors who wish to include such basic needs statements: See "Basic Needs Syllabus Integration," Open CoLab, accessed May 1, 2023, https://colab.plymouthcreate.net/ace/ace-practice /basic-needs-and-gateless-policies-syllabus/. Many campuses now provide sample language for a basic needs statement, such as the Department of Women and Gender Studies at the University of Colorado Boulder ("'Basic Needs' Syllabus Statement," https://www.colorado.edu/wgst/basic-needs-syllabus-statement), Grinnell (Samuel A. Rebelsky, "Adding a Basic Needs Statement to the Course Syllabus," *SamR's Assorted Musings and Rants* [blog], https://rebelsky.cs .grinnell.edu/musings/basic-needs-syllabus), and Central Oregon Community College ("Basic Needs Syllabus Statement," Central Oregon Community College, https://www.cocc.edu/departments/step/basic-needs-statement.aspx), all accessed May 1, 2023.

13. I know I am guilty of this. I once gave a presentation to the local genealogical society about the Irish in America and began my talk with the Norman— or Anglo-Norman, or Cambro-Norman (there is a debate)—invasion of Ireland in 1169.

14. For a concise summary of objections to learning goals and arguments for them, see "On Learning Goals and Learning Objectives," Derek Bok Center for Teaching and Learning, Harvard University, accessed May 1, 2023, https:// bokcenter.harvard.edu/learning-goals-and-learning-objectives.

15. See Jesse Stommel, "My favorite 'learning outcomes' apply . . . ," Twitter (now X), October 22, 2019, https://twitter.com/Jessifer/status/118667 8693063745538.

16. Although I fumbled my way to these questions on my own, I was reinventing the wheel. This approach is called Backward Design, and perhaps its best articulation can be found in Grant Wiggins and Jay McTighe, *Understanding by Design*, 2nd ed. (Alexandria, VA: Association for Supervision and Curriculum Development, 2005.)

17. It has been well established that students welcome images and graphic organizers in syllabi and rate them highly. (Don't forget to embed alt text in any visuals you use.) See Harrington and Gabert-Quillen, "Syllabus Length," 2, 7–8.

18. See Canva, http://www.canva.com; Venngage, http://venngage.com; Pexels, http://www.pexels.com; Freepik, http://www.freepik.com; Flaticon, http:// www.flaticon.com; and Storyset, http://storyset.com.

19. Open Sans is available as a standard font in Google docs. Lexie Readable is available for download at https://www.k-type.com/fonts/lexie-readable/ and Atkinson Hyperlegible is available for download at https://brailleinstitute .org/freefont; both accessed May 1, 2023.

20. The National Eye Institute estimates that one in twelve men suffer from color vision deficiency. See "Color Blindness," National Eye Institute, updated August 11, 2023, https://www.nei.nih.gov/learn-about-eye-health/eye-conditions-and-diseases/color-blindness.

21. I'm grateful to Karen Costa, Judith Dutill, Clea Mahoney, and Melissa Wehler for their instruction on these approaches. All these recommendations are inspired by Universal Design for Learning. For more on UDL, see Thomas J. Tobin and Kristen Behling, *Reach Everyone, Teach Everyone: Universal Design for Learning in Higher Education* (Morgantown: West Virginia University Press, 2018); Lillian Nave, *Think UDL* (podcast), various dates, accessed May 1, 2023, https://thinkudl.org/; and "The UDL Guidelines," CAST, accessed May 1, 2023, https://udlguidelines.cast.org/. UDL is sometimes oversimplified, and it's important to think about its complexities. See Jay Dolmage, "Universal Design: Places to Start," *Disability Studies Quarterly* 35, no. 2 (2015), https://dsq-sds.org/article/view/4632/3946.

22. Ann Gagné, "Episode Six: Accessible Word and PDF Documents," *Accessagogy* (podcast), April 18, 2023, https://anngagne.ca/podcast/episode-6-accessible-word-and-pdf-documents/.

23. For a short but thorough introduction to metacognition, see Nancy Chick, "Metacognition," Vanderbilt University Center for Teaching, 2013, https://cft.vanderbilt.edu/guides-sub-pages/metacognition/.

24. Facebook Messenger conversation with Courtney Pletcher, March 20, 2023. Copy in author's possession.

25. Text conversation with Kylie Hoang, March 20, 2023. Copy in author's possession.

26. Remi Kalir, "Annotate Your Syllabus, 4.0.," *Remi(x)learning* (blog), August 8, 2022, https://remikalir.com/blog/annotate-your-syllabus-4-0/.

27. Ashley Mowreader, "Academic Success Tip: Help Students Excel at Organization," Inside Higher Ed, March 16, 2023, https://www.insidehighered.com/news/2023/03/17/academic-coaches-organize-student-deadlines.

28. Caleb McDaniel, "Generic Syllabus Maker," Rice University, accessed May 1, 2023, http://wcaleb.rice.edu/syllabusmaker/generic/.

Chapter 3. Kindness and Assessment

1. Conversation with Clarissa Sorensen-Unruh through Twitter direct messages, September 26, 2022. Text of full conversation in possession of author.

2. Jordynn Jack and Viji Sathy, "It's Time to Cancel the Word Rigor," *Chronicle of Higher Education*, September 24, 2021, https://www.chronicle.com/article/its-time-to-cancel-the-word-rigor.

3. Deborah J. Cohan, "Upholding Rigor at Pandemic U," Inside Higher Ed, August 24, 2021, https://www.insidehighered.com/advice/2021/08/25

/professors-should-uphold-rigor-when-assessing-students-even-pandemic
-opinion; and David Syphers, "In Defense of Rigor," Inside Higher Ed, September 22, 2021, https://www.insidehighered.com/views/2021/09/22/why-rigor
-instruction-matters.

4. Jack and Sathy, "It's Time to Cancel."

5. See, for example, Alex J. Novikoff, *The Medieval Culture of Disputation: Pedagogy, Practice, and Performance* (Philadelphia: University of Pennsylvania Press, 2013); Mary Carruthers, *The Book of Memory: A Study of Memory in Medieval Culture*, 2nd ed. (Cambridge: Cambridge University Press, 2008); and Hilde de Ridder-Symoens, ed., *A History of the University in Europe*, Vol. 1: *Universities in the Middle Ages* (Cambridge: Cambridge University Press, 1992).

6. For a sampling of texts that emphasize the importance of oral history and tradition, see Keith Basso, *Wisdom Sits in Places: Landscape and Language among the Western Apache* (Albuquerque: University of New Mexico Press, 1996); Waziyatawin Angela Wilson, *Remember This! Dakota Decolonization and the Eli Taylor Narratives* (Lincoln: University of Nebraska Press, 2005); Shawn Wilson, *Research Is Ceremony: Indigenous Research Methods* (Halifax, Nova Scotia: Fernwood, 2008); Aubrey Jean Hanson, *Literatures, Communities, and Learning: Conversations with Indigenous Writers* (Waterloo, Ontario: Wilfred Laurier University Press, 2020); Jan Vansina, *Paths in the Rainforest: Toward a History of Political Tradition in Equatorial Africa* (Madison: University of Wisconsin Press, 1990); Luise White, *Speaking with Vampires: Rumor and History in Colonial Africa* (Oakland: University of California Press, 2000); and Luise White, Stephan F. Miescher, and David William Cohen, eds., *African Words, African Voices: Critical Practices in Oral History* (Bloomington: Indiana University Press, 2001).

7. This does not even get into the many ways in which history might be offered to and interpreted by various groups. Museums, monuments, galleries, historic sites—these are all places that communicate history in a variety of mediums. Music, documentaries, novels, fictional films—there are a host of ways in which someone might receive and conceive of history.

8. Jay T. Dolmage, *Academic Ableism: Disability and Higher Education* (Ann Arbor: University of Michigan Press, 2017); Margaret Price, *Mad at School: Rhetorics of Mental Disability and Academic Life* (Ann Arbor: University of Michigan Press, 2011); and Johanna Schoen, *Choice and Coercion: Birth Control, Sterilization, and Abortion in Public Health and Welfare* (Chapel Hill: University of North Carolina Press, 2005).

9. Allie Grasgreen, "Dropping the Ball on Disabilities," Inside Higher Ed, April 1, 2014, https://www.insidehighered.com/news/2014/04/02/students
-disabilities-frustrated-ignorance-and-lack-services; Lennard J. Davis, "Where's the Outrage When Colleges Discriminate against Students with Disabilities?," *Chronicle of Higher Education*, July 23, 2015, https://www.chronicle.com
/article/wheres-the-outrage-when-colleges-discriminate-against-students-with
-disabilities/; Jessica Bursztynsky, "UI Professor Leaves after Email Scandal

Refusing to Accommodate Student," *Daily Illini*, September 12, 2017, https://dailyillini.com/news-stories/campus-life/2017/09/12/ui-professor-leaves-refusing-accommodate-student/; and Mia Rasamny, "A Clear Violation of the Law," *Hoya*, February 4, 2022, https://thehoya.com/a-clear-violation-of-the-law-professors-reject-student-disability-accommodations/.

10. "Americans with Disabilities Act Title II Regulations," Subpart B, § 35:130 (a) and (b) (7) i, October 11, 2016, https://www.ada.gov/regs2010/titleII_2010/titleII_2010_regulations.htm.

11. For more examples, see Sonny Jane Wise's neurodivergent umbrella on Instagram, December 28, 2021, https://www.instagram.com/p/CYBl-miPcCL/?hl=en.

12. It cannot be said loudly enough: access for disabled people improves access for everyone. For more examples of this truth, see Rachel Kang, "The Journey to Accessible Apps," *Xamarin* (Microsoft Developer blog), April 14, 2021, https://devblogs.microsoft.com/xamarin/the-journey-to-accessible-apps/.

13. Philip Galanes, "Is Extra Help Hurting My Friend with Autism?," *New York Times*, April 19, 2018, https://www.nytimes.com/2018/04/19/style/is-extra-help-hurting-my-friend-with-autism.html.

14. Devon Frye, "The Children Left Behind," *ADDitude*, March 31, 2022, https://www.additudemag.com/race-and-adhd-how-people-of-color-get-left-behind/; Paul L. Morgan et al., "Racial and Ethnic Disparities in ADHD Diagnosis from Kindergarten to Eighth Grade," *Pediatrics* 132, no. 1 (July 2013): 85–93, https://doi.org/10.1542/peds.2012-2390; Stephen P. Hinshaw et al., "Annual Research Review: Attention Deficit/Hyperactivity in Girls and Women: Underrepresentation, Longitudinal Processes, and Key Directions," *Journal of Child Psychology and Psychiatry* 63, no. 4 (April 2022): 484–96, https://doi.org/10.1111/jcpp.13480; and Andrea Chronis-Tuscano, "ADHD in Girls and Women: A Call to Action—Reflections on Hinshaw et al. (2021)," *Journal of Child Psychology and Psychiatry* 63, no. 4 (April 2022): 497–99, https://doi.org/10.1111/jcpp.13574. Conversely, there are many people who are forced to self-diagnose because of financial, logistical, temporal, physical, and other structural obstacles to them receiving a medical diagnosis, or who choose it as a means of resisting the ableist dictates of the medical establishment. See, for example, Devon Price, *Unmasking Autism: Discovering the New Faces of Neurodiversity* (New York: Harmony, 2022), 45–46.

15. Devon Price, *Laziness Does Not Exist* (New York: Simon & Schuster, 2022).

16. Thomas J. Tobin and Kirsten T. Behling, *Reach Everyone, Teach Everyone: Universal Design for Learning in Higher Education* (Morgantown: West Virginia University Press, 2018), 25.

17. Tobin and Behling, *Reach Everyone*, 134.

18. It's important to note that there are learning curves involved in changing our assessment practices and utilizing new technology. Recording an audio

clip may take us more time than we're used to spending on feedback, especially at first. But my experience has been that, as with most things, practice and repetition translates into efficacy. Still, allow yourself time to experiment with new technology before applying it in class, or use it in a small-class setting the first time around.

19. In addition to Tobin and Behling, see, for example, Sheryl E Burgstahler, ed., *Universal Design in Higher Education: From Principles to Practice* (Cambridge, MA: Harvard University Press, 2015); Jennifer L. Pusateri, *Transform Your Teaching with Universal Design: Six Steps to Jumpstart Your Practice* (Wakefield, MA: CAST, 2022); and "The UDL Guidelines," CAST, accessed May 2, 2023, https://udlguidelines.cast.org/.

20. Daniel Paul O'Donnell, "The Unessay," *Daniel Paul O'Donnell* (blog), last modified September 28, 2018, https://people.uleth.ca/~daniel.odonnell/Teaching/the-unessay.

21. I first learned about unessays from Christopher Jones, who shared some student work on Twitter on December 11, 2017, https://twitter.com/ccjones13/status/940329059073982464. I'm also grateful to Jessamyn Neuhaus, Jacqueline Antonovich, Aparna Nair, and Jessica Derleth, who have used unessays to incredible effect.

22. Munir Fasheh, "The Trouble with Knowledge," Shikshantar: The People's Institute for Re-thinking Education and Development, accessed May 2, 2023, https://shikshantar.org/articles/trouble-knowledge.

23. Leslie Berntsen, "How Not to Handle Student Failure," *Chronicle of Higher Education*, October 13, 2022, https://www.chronicle.com/article/how-not-to-handle-student-failure.

24. If you're interested in how the A-to-F system took hold in the United States, see Jeffrey Schinske and Kimberley Tanner, "Teaching by Grading Less (or Differently)," *CBE—Life Sciences Education* 13, no. 2 (Summer 2014): 159–66, https://doi.org/10.1187/cbe.cbe-14-03-0054. For more on the history of grades see Mark W. Durm, "An A Is Not an A: A History of Grading," *Educational Forum* 57, no. 3 (1993): 294–97, https://doi.org/10.1080/00131729309335429.

25. See Susan D. Blum, "Why Ungrade? Why Grade?," in *Ungrading: Why Rating Students Undermines Learning (and What to Do Instead)* (Morgantown: West Virginia University Press, 2020), 10–12. Some instructors curve the grade returns in their classes with the aim of providing consistency, but as Schinske and Tanner write, "even if we were to accept a concept of innate aptitude that is normally distributed in a classroom, that distribution should not predict classroom achievement, provided the class environment supports diverse learners in appropriate ways." Schinske and Tanner, "Teaching by Grading Less," 162.

26. For a vital reflection on the importance of systems and structure for neuro-divergent learners, see Karen Ray Costa, "Systems Aren't Scary," Medium,

October 31, 2022, https://karenraycosta.medium.com/systems-arent-scary
-e55d8ac63bc7.

27. Schinske and Tanner, "Teaching by Grading Less," 161. See also Alfie
Kohn, "The Case Against Grades," Alfie Kohn, November 2011, https://www
.alfiekohn.org/article/case-grades/.

28. Lindsay C. Masland, "Ungrading: The Joys of Doing Everything
Wrong," *Zeal: A Journal for the Liberal Arts* 1, no. 2 (2023): 89. Katie Mattaini
offers a succinct summary of the multiple definitions of "ungrading" in circulation on Twitter, May 1, 2023, https://twitter.com/katiemattaini/status
/1653085092623925277.

29. John Warner, "There's No Right Way to Ungrade," Inside Higher Ed,
October 24, 2022, https://www.insidehighered.com/blogs/just-visiting/there
%E2%80%99s-no-right-way-ungrade.

30. Jesse Stommel, "How to Ungrade," Jesse Stommel, March 11, 2018,
https://www.jessestommel.com/how-to-ungrade/.

31. Cate Denial, "Making the Grade," *Cate Denial* (blog), October 16, 2017,
https://catherinedenial.org/blog/uncategorized/making-the-grade/.

32. By the time students reach college, they are primed to see red ink signaling their failings. Consider responding to your students in some other color,
or even in pencil, or using comment features on electronic files. It's a small
kindness that can make a big difference in how your feedback is received.

33. For excellent, mid-process reflections on ungrading, see Maha Bali,
"Reflections on Ungrading for the 4th Time," *Reflecting Allowed* (blog), March 23,
2019, https://blog.mahabali.me/pedagogy/reflections-on-ungrading-for-the-4th
-time/; Stephanie Jennings, "Ungrading: A Review, a Retrospective, a Messy Path
Ahead," Michigan State University, College of Education, Digital Instruction Support Community, July 21, 2021, https://education.msu.edu/digital-instruction
-support-community/uncategorized/ungrading-a-review-a-retrospective-a-messy
-path-ahead/; "Chart a Course: Ungrading with Courtney Sobers," Rutgers
School of Arts & Sciences–Newark, YouTube, 2021, https://www.youtube.com
/watch?v=YadoqOs6UpA; and Laila I. McCloud, "Keeping Receipts: Thoughts on
Ungrading from a Black Woman Professor," *Zeal: A Journal for the Liberal Arts* 1,
no. 2 (April 2023): 101–5.

34. Cate Denial, "Going Gradeless," *Cate Denial* (blog), June 10, 2022,
https://catherinedenial.org/blog/uncategorized/going-gradeless/. Not all students are ready to self-assess without help. For more discussion of inequities and
ungrading, see Beckie Supiano, "The Unintended Consequences of 'Ungrading':
Does Getting Rid of Grades Make Things Worse for Disadvantaged Students?,"
Chronicle of Higher Education, April 29, 2022, https://www.chronicle.com/article
/the-unintended-consequences-of-ungrading.

35. Gary Chu, "The Point-Less Classroom: A Math Teacher's Ironic Choice
in Not Calculating Grades," in Blum, *Ungrading*, 167.

36. Chu, 161–70, and Clarissa Sorensen-Unruh, "A STEM Ungrading Case Study: A Reflection on First-Time Implementation in Organic Chemistry II," in Blum, *Ungrading*, 140–60.

37. Heather Miceli, "Ungrading in a General Education Science Course," June 11, 2021, in David Buck, ed., *Crowdsourcing Ungrading*, Pressbooks, convened 2020, https://pressbooks.howardcc.edu/ungrading/chapter/ungrading-in -a-general-education-science-course/.

38. See, for example, Beth McMurtrie, "A 'Stunning' Level of Student Disconnection," *Chronicle of Higher Education*, April 5, 2022, https://www.chronicle.com /article/a-stunning-level-of-student-disconnection; and Rebecca A. Glazier et al., "How to Solve the Student-Disengagement Crisis: Six Experts Diagnose the Problem—and Suggest Ways to Fix It," *Chronicle of Higher Education*, May 11, 2022, https://www.chronicle.com/article/how-to-solve-the-student-disengagement -crisis.

39. Cate Denial, Clarissa Sorensen-Unruh, and Elizabeth A. Lehfeldt, "After the Pivot Should Come the Great Pause," *Chronicle of Higher Education*, February 25, 2022, https://www.chronicle.com/article/after-the-great-pivot -should-come-the-great-pause; and Steven Mintz, "An Epidemic of Student Disengagement: Eight Ways to Re-Engage Disconnected College Students," Inside Higher Ed, April 13, 2022, https://www.insidehighered.com/blogs/higher-ed -gamma/epidemic-student-disengagement.

40. Future Forum has an archive of multiple reports on how the pandemic has reshaped the working world: "Research: Our Findings on the Future of Work," Future Forum, Summer 2021-Winter 2023, https://futureforum.com /research/. For an interview that summarizes some of their work, see Anne Helen Petersen, "Why Are Bosses So Miserable?: Talking About the Future of Work with Sheela Subramanian," *Culture Study* (blog), October 20, 2022, https:// annehelen.substack.com/p/why-are-bosses-so-miserable. See also Anne Helen Petersen, "So You've Decided to Bungle your Company's Flexible Work Plan: The Four Most Popular Bungles and Four Very Straightforward Alternatives," *Culture Study* (blog), July 6, 2022, https://annehelen.substack.com/p/so-youve-decided -to-bungle-your-companys. On students, see Karen Costa, "The Desire Path of Empty Classrooms," Medium, December 1, 2022, https://karenraycosta.medium .com/the-desire-path-of-empty-classrooms-72d7cc9f103d; and "Trauma Aware Pedagogy," *Tea for Teaching* (podcast), June 8, 2022, https://teaforteaching.com /243-trauma-aware-pedagogy/.

41. "TILT Higher Ed Examples and Resources," TILT Higher Ed, accessed May 2, 2023, https://tilthighered.com/tiltexamplesandresources.

42. For an in-depth dive into the importance of structure in teaching and learning, see Kelly A. Hogan and Viji Sathy, "The Value of Structure," in *Inclusive Teaching: Strategies for Promoting Equity in the College Classroom* (Morgantown: West Virginia University Press, 2022), 27–48.

43. Stommel, "How to Ungrade."
44. Sathy and Hogan, "The Value of Structure," 19.

Chapter 4. Kindness in the Classroom

1. Maha Bali et al., "Intentionally Equitable Hospitality in Hybrid Video Dialogue: The Context of Virtually Connecting," *eLearn* 5, no. 5 (May 2019), https://doi.org/10.1145/3329488.3331173.

2. Maha Bali and Mia Zamora, "Intentionally Equitable Hospitality as Critical Instructional Design," in Jerod Quinn and Martha Burtis, eds., *Designing for Care* (Hybrid Pedagogy, Inc.: 2022), accessed May 2, 2023, https://pressbooks.pub/designingforcare/chapter/intentionally-equitable-hospitality-as-critical-instructional-design/.

3. "The Big List of Self-Care Activities" (adapted from Matthew McKay, Jeffrey C. Wood, and Jeffrey Brantley, *The Dialectical Behavior Therapy Skills Workbook* [Oakland, CA: New Harbinger, 2007]), Indiana Youth Institute, accessed May 2, 2023, https://www.iyi.org/wp-content/uploads/2020/02/Additional-Referenced-Resources.pdf; "Coloring Pages for Adults," Just Color, 2023, https://www.justcolor.net/; and "Everything Is Awful and I'm Not Okay: Questions to Ask before Giving Up," University of Washington, accessed May 2, 2023, https://depts.washington.edu/fammed/wp-content/uploads/2019/03/Katers-selfcare_printable.pdf.

4. "Self-Care Inventory" (adapted from Child Welfare Training Toolkit, March 2008; original source unknown), National Alliance on Mental Illness, accessed May 2, 2023, https://www.nami.org/NAMI/media/Extranet-Education/HF15AR6SelfCare.pdf; and "Assessing Your Life Balance" (from R. Robertson and G. Microys, *Life Balance Assessment and Action Planning Guide* [2001–2] and Lutheran Social Services of Michigan, *Your Guide to the Wellness Wheel*), University of California, Irvine, accessed May 2, 2023, https://studentwellness.uci.edu/wp-content/uploads/2015/04/Assessing-Your-Life-Balance.pdf.

5. Devon Price, "Laziness Does Not Exist," Medium, March 23, 2018, https://humanparts.medium.com/laziness-does-not-exist-3af27e312d01; "Read Aloud: Voice Enabling the Web," accessed May 2, 2023, https://readaloud.app/.

6. Michelle Pacansky-Brock, "Humanizing Pre-course Contact with a Liquid Syllabus," Brocansky.com, June 9, 2020, https://brocansky.com/2020/06/humanizing-pre-course-contact-with-a-liquid-syllabus.html. A version of her liquid syllabus welcome package for History of Still Photo, an eight-week online course that began on January 17, 2023, can be found at https://sites.google.com/view/hosp-welcome, accessed May 2, 2023.

7. Hogan and Sathy also offer sample questions to include in such a survey. See Kelly A. Hogan and Viji Sathy, *Inclusive Teaching: Strategies for Promoting*

Equity in the College Classroom (Morgantown: West Virginia University Press, 2022), 88–89.

8. Karen Costa, "Systems Aren't Scary," Medium, October 31, 2022, https://karenraycosta.medium.com/systems-arent-scary-e55d8ac63bc7.

9. Hogan and Sathy offer a host of great suggestions for what to do before a particular class period starts, including the idea of circulating among the students. See *Inclusive Teaching*, 91.

10. Mary Rose O'Reilley, *Radical Presence: Teaching as Contemplative Practice* (Portsmouth, NH: Boynton/Cook Publishers, 1998), 8.

11. O'Reilley, *Radical Presence*, 8.

12. I do not require my students to share their pronouns, as I do not wish to cause distress and discomfort to students who are transitioning or who don't wish to out themselves but do wish to answer such questions honestly. See, for example, Rachel N. Levin, "The Problem with Pronouns," Inside Higher Ed, September 18, 2018, https://www.insidehighered.com/views/2018/09/19/why-asking-students-their-preferred-pronoun-not-good-idea-opinion; Olive L. Haimson and Lee Airton, "Making Space for Them, Her, Him, and 'Prefer Not to Disclose' in Group Settings: Why Pronoun-Sharing Is Important but Must Remain Optional," National Center for Institutional Diversity, June 4, 2018, https://medium.com/national-center-for-institutional-diversity/making-space-for-them-her-him-and-prefer-not-to-disclose-in-group-settings-why-1deb8c3d6b86; and Ed Plowe, "Don't Ask Me for My Pronouns Yet," *Cornell Daily Sun*, August 30, 2022, https://cornellsun.com/2022/08/30/plowe-dont-ask-me-for-my-pronouns-yet/. I do, however, model pronoun use by sharing my own, a practice that researchers Aditi Kodipady and colleagues call "norm support": affirming both the act of sharing pronouns when comfortable and the fact that there are multiple genders in the world. Aditi Kodipady et al., "Beyond Virtue Signaling: Perceived Motivations for Pronoun Sharing," *Journal of Applied Social Psychology* (October 2022): 1–18, https://doi.org/10.1111/jasp.12937.

13. This question is suggested by Mary Rose O'Reilley in *Radical Presence*, page 9.

14. Katherine Isbister, "Fidget Toys Aren't Just Hype," The Conversation, May 17, 2017, https://theconversation.com/fidget-toys-arent-just-hype-77456.

15. Colleen Flaherty, "What Students Want (and Don't) from Their Professors," Inside Higher Ed, March 23, 2023, https://www.insidehighered.com/news/2023/03/24/survey-faculty-teaching-style-impedes-academic-success-students-say. See also Brandi N. Frisby and Matthew M. Martin, "Instructor-Student and Student-Student Rapport in the Classroom," *Communication Education* 59, no. 2 (2010): 146–64, https://doi.org/10.1080/03634520903564362; Nathan G. Webb and Laura Obrycki Barrett, "Student Views of Instructor-Student Rapport in the College Classroom," *Journal of the Scholarship of Teaching and Learning* 14, no. 2 (2014): 15–28, https://doi.org/10.14434/josotl.v14i2.4259; and William J. Lammers and J. Arthur Gillaspy Jr., "Brief Measure of Student-Instructor Rapport

Predicts Student Success in Online Classes," *International Journal for the Scholarship of Teaching and Learning* 7, no. 2 (2013), article 16, https://doi.org/10.20429 /ijsotl.2013.070216. On naming, specifically, see Molly Townes O'Brien, Tania Leiman, and James Duffy, "The Power of Naming: The Multifaceted Value of Learning Students' Names," *QUT Law Review* 14, no. 1 (2014): 114–28, https:// doi.org/10.5204/qutlr.v14i1.544; and Katelyn M. Cooper et al., "What's in a Name?: The Importance of Students Perceiving That an Instructor Knows Their Names in a High-Enrollment Biology Classroom," *CBE—Life Sciences Education* 16, no. 1 (Spring 2017): 1–13, https://doi.org/10.1187/cbe.16-08-0265.

16. For other suggestions related to learning names, see "Tips for Learning Student Names," Teaching and Learning Resource Center, Ohio State University, accessed May 2, 2023, https://teaching.resources.osu.edu/examples/tips -learning-student-names.

17. For examples, see Janis Meredith, "100 Would You Rather . . . Questions," SignUp Genius, accessed May 22, 2023, https://www.signupgenius.com /groups/would-you-rather.cfm; and "250 Best 'Would You Rather' Questions to Learn More about Friends Than You Ever Expected," Parade, May 22, 2023, https://parade.com/964027/parade/would-you-rather-questions/.

18. I do not ask students to tell me what their names mean, as student comfort with that question varies widely, especially when students are adopted or engaged in gender transition. Instead, by asking for a story related to their name, they can define the parameters of what they share. My own last name can be traced back to an infant boy who was left on the steps of Norton Parish Church on what's now the south side of Sheffield, England, in the 1740s. The vicar found the boy and asked every woman in the village if he was theirs. They all said no, and the vicar adopted the boy and called him Daniel Denial.

19. "Introductory Activities: Creative Ways to Do Student Introductions on Your First Week of Classes," OneHE, accessed May 2, 2023, https://onehe.org /equity-unbound/introductory-activities/.

20. sarah madoka currie, "the mad manifesto" (PhD diss., University of Waterloo, 2023), 245, https://uwspace.uwaterloo.ca/bitstream/handle/10012 /19689/Currie_Sarah.pdf?sequence=3&isAllowed=y.

21. For student analysis of this group structure, see sarah madoka currie and the students of W2022 ENGL 109-007, "beyond the community tradition: conjuring community-first syllabi in apocalypse time," *Spark: A 4C4Equality Journal*, vol. 4, April 19, 2022, https://sparkactivism.com/beyond-the-ability -tradition/.

22. For examples, see Cynthia J. Brame and Rachel Biel, "Group Work: Using Cooperative Learning Groups Effectively," Center for Teaching, Vanderbilt University, 2015, https://cft.vanderbilt.edu/guides-sub-pages/setting-up-and -facilitating-group-work-using-cooperative-learning-groups-effectively/; "How to Create and Manage Groups," Center for Teaching Innovation, Cornell University, accessed May 2, 2023, https://teaching.cornell.edu/teaching-resources

/active-collaborative-learning/how-create-and-manage-groups; and "What are Best Practices for Designing Group Projects?," Eberly Center, Carnegie Mellon University, accessed May 2, 2023, https://www.cmu.edu/teaching/designteach /teach/instructionalstrategies/groupprojects/design.html.

23. These last four relate to learning experiences involving students I taught in 2022.

24. Joshua R. Eyler, "Discussion-Based Pedagogies," in *How Humans Learn: The Science and Stories Behind Effective College Teaching* (Morgantown: University of West Virginia Press, 2018), 45–48; and Kelly H. Hogan and Viji Sathy, "Classroom Environment and Interactions," in *Inclusive Teaching: Strategies for Promoting Equity in the College Classroom* (Morgantown: University of West Virginia Press, 2022), 107–57.

25. Brenna Clarke Gray, "Five Conversations about Education I Would Rather Eat Glass Than Continue Having," *Little EdTech, Big Mouth* (blog), November 10, 2022, https://blog.brennaclarkegray.ca/2022/11/10/five-conversations -about-education-i-would-rather-eat-glass-than-continue-having/.

26. See Catherine Denial and Gabrielle Raley-Karlin, "Ground Rules for Dialogue," adapted from "Ground Rules" from the Program on Intergroup Relations at the University of Michigan. Copies available from the author upon request. For a sample handout from the University of Michigan, go to https://igr .umich.edu/IGR-Insight-Handouts, accessed May 2, 2023.

27. For a wonderful in-depth discussion of classroom participation, see Hogan and Sathy, *Inclusive Teaching*, 107–57.

28. Derek Bruff, "In Defense of Continuous Exposition by the Teacher," *Agile Learning* (blog), September 15, 2015, https://derekbruff.org/?p=3126; Joshua R. Eyler, "The Inauthenticity of the Lecture," in *How Humans Learn: The Science and Stories behind Effective College Teaching* (Morgantown: West Virginia University Press, 2018), 164–68; Scott Freeman et al., "Active Learning Increases Student Performance in Science, Engineering, and Mathematics," *Psychological and Cognitive Sciences* 111, no. 23 (2014): 8410–15, https://doi.org/10.1073/pnas .1319030111; and Thomas Buchanan and Edward Palmer, "Student Perceptions of the History Lecture: Does This Delivery Mode Have a Future in the Humanities?," *Journal of University Learning & Teaching Practice* 14, no. 2 (2017), https:// doi.org/10.53761/1.14.2.4, at https://ro.uow.edu.au/cgi/viewcontent.cgi?article= 1701&context=jutlp. For a defense of the lecture, see Molly Worthen, "Lecture Me. Really," *New York Times*, October 17, 2015.

29. See Mentimeter, https://www.mentimeter.com/education; Poll Everywhere, https://www.polleverywhere.com/mobile; and Slido, https://www.slido .com/?experience_id=15-a, all accessed May 2, 2023.

30. See, for example, on the *Catherine Denial* blog: "The Art of the Draw," October 16, 2019, https://catherinedenial.org/blog/uncategorized/the-art-of -the-draw/; and "Human Asset Maps: Encouraging Social Justice Work in My

Students," January 22, 2017, https://catherinedenial.org/blog/uncategorized /human-asset-maps-encouraging-social-justice-work-in-my-students/.

31. Catherine J. Denial, "Atoms, Honeycombs, and Fabric Scraps: Rethinking Timelines in the Undergraduate Classroom," *History Teacher* 46, no. 3 (May 2013): 415–34, https://www.jstor.org/stable/43264133.

32. For sample handouts for this practice, see Cate Denial, "Strong Emotional Reactions," *Cate Denial* (blog), December 10, 2018, https://catherinedenial .org/blog/uncategorized/strong-emotional-reactions/.

33. Robert R. Stains, Jr., and John Sarrouf, "Hard to Say; Hard to Hear; Heart to Heart: Inviting and Harnessing Strong Emotions in Dialogue for Deliberation," *Journal of Deliberative Democracy* 18, no. 2 (2022): 3, https://doi.org/10 .16997/jdd.979.

34. *Responding to Triggers* (video and transcript), excerpt from Community Organizing for Social Justice (course), Michigan Online, accessed May 2, 2023, https://online.umich.edu/collections/racism-antiracism/short/responding -triggers/.

35. *Responding to Triggers.*

36. "IGR Insight Handouts," Program on Intergroup Relations, University of Michigan, accessed May 2, 2023, https://igr.umich.edu/IGR-Insight-Handouts; "Managing Difficult Classroom Conversations," Center for Innovative Teaching and Learning, Indiana University Bloomington, accessed May 2, 2023, https:// citl.indiana.edu/teaching-resources/diversity-inclusion/managing-difficult -classroom-discussions/index.html; "CRP Resources," Center for Restorative Practices, Amherst College, accessed May 2, 2023, https://www.amherst.edu/offices /restorative-practices/rpac-reading-list; and "Navigating Difficult Moments," Derek Bok Center for Teaching and Learning, Harvard University, accessed May 2, 2023, https://bokcenter.harvard.edu/navigating-difficult-moments.

37. Danya Ruttenberg, *On Repentance and Repair: Making Amends in an Unapologetic World* (Boston: Beacon Press, 2022), 3–4.

38. See Ruttenberg, *On Repentance and Repair*, "Introduction," particularly pages 15–16.

39. A recent study was widely hailed as proving that content/trigger warnings were not at all helpful to students, but by the authors' own admission, "researchers did not specifically recruit people with a history of psychopathology," thereby excluding those students for whom warnings are designed. Colleen Flaherty, "Death Knell for Trigger Warnings?," Inside Higher Ed, March 20, 2019, https:// www.insidehighered.com/news/2019/03/21/new-study-says-trigger-warnings -are-useless-does-mean-they-should-be-abandoned; Mevagh Sanson, Deryn Strange, and Maryanne Garry, "Trigger Warnings Are Trivially Helpful at Reducing Negative Affect, Intrusive Thoughts, and Avoidance," *Clinical Psychological Science* 7, no. 4 (2019): 778–93, https://doi.org/10.1177/2167702619827018; and Amna Khalid and Jeffrey Aaron Snyder, "The Data Is In—Trigger Warnings Don't

Work," *Chronicle of Higher Education*, September 15, 2021, https://www.chronicle
.com/article/the-data-is-in-trigger-warnings-dont-work.

40. Staci K. Haines, *The Politics of Trauma: Somatics, Healing, and Social
Justice* (Berkeley, CA: North Atlantic Books, 2019); and Mays Imad, "Our Brains,
Emotions, and Learning: Eight Principles of Trauma-Informed Teaching,"
in Phyllis Thompson and Janice Carello, eds., *Trauma-Informed Pedagogies: A
Guide for Responding to Crisis and Inequality in Higher Education* (New York: Palgrave Macmillan, 2022), 35–47. For a description of my own experience when
triggered, see Cate Denial, "On Being Triggered," *Cate Denial* (blog), March 9,
2017, https://catherinedenial.org/blog/uncategorized/on-being-triggered/.

41. For data on the vast inequities in mental health services in the United
States, for example, see "Behavioral Health Equity," SAMHSA (Substance Abuse
and Mental Health Services Administration), accessed May 2, 2023, https://www
.samhsa.gov/behavioral-health-equity/resources.

42. I have heard individuals assert that surely exposure to difficult material
is therapeutically beneficial for traumatized students. In order: (1) We are not
our students' therapists; (2) exposure therapy is not the only or even the best
treatment for every person; and (3) our classrooms are not therapeutic spaces.
Do not do this.

Conclusion

1. Robert F. Kennedy, "Day of Affirmation Address, University of Cape
Town, Cape Town, South Africa, June 6, 1966," John F. Kennedy Presidential
Library and Museum, https://www.jfklibrary.org/learn/about-jfk/the-kennedy
-family/robert-f-kennedy/robert-f-kennedy-speeches/day-of-affirmation-address
-university-of-capetown-capetown-south-africa-june-6-1966.

BIBLIOGRAPHY

AAUP (American Association of University Professors). "Background Facts on Contingent Faculty Positions." Accessed April 29, 2023. https://www.aaup .org/issues/contingency/background-facts.

Abril, Danielle. "Ask Help Desk: How Remote Workers Can Separate Home and Work Lives." *Washington Post*, October 29, 2021. https://www.washingtonpost .com/technology/2021/10/29/ask-help-desk-remote-work-return-to-office -tablets-laptops/.

American Psychological Association. "Campus Sexual Assault and Campus Climate." Last updated July 2019. https://www.apa.org/advocacy/interpersonal -violence/sexual-assault-campus-climate.pdf.

American Studies Association, "Resolution on Defending Academic Freedom Against Attacks on 'Critical Race Theory,'" posted February 10, 2022. https:// www.theasa.net/about/news-events/announcements/resolution-defending -academic-freedom-against-attacks-%E2%80%9Ccritical-race.

"Americans with Disabilities Act Title II Regulations," Subpart B, § 35:130 (a) and (b) (7) i, October 11, 2016. https://www.ada.gov/regs2010/titleII_2010/titleII _2010_regulations.htm.

Amherst College, Center for Restorative Practices. "CRP Resources." Accessed May 2, 2023. https://www.amherst.edu/offices/restorative-practices/rpac -reading-list.

Anderson, Jenny. "The Only Metric of Success That Really Matters Is the One We Ignore." Quartz, March 12, 2019. https://qz.com/1570179/how-to-make -friends-build-a-community-and-create-the-life-you-want/.

"Anti-Muslim Hatred Has Reached 'Epidemic Proportions' Says UN Rights Expert, Urging Action by States." United Nations, March 4, 2021. https:// news.un.org/en/story/2021/03/1086452.

"Assessing Your Life Balance" (from R. Robertson and G. Microys, *Life Balance Assessment and Action Planning Guide* [2001–2] and Lutheran Social Services of Michigan, *Your Guide to the Wellness Wheel*). University of California, Irvine. Accessed May 2, 2023. https://studentwellness.uci.edu/wp-content/uploads /2015/04/Assessing-Your-Life-Balance.pdf.

Bali, Maha. "Reflections on Ungrading for the 4th Time." *Reflecting Allowed* (blog), March 23, 2019. https://blog.mahabali.me/pedagogy/reflections-on -ungrading-for-the-4th-time/.

Bali, Maha, and Mia Zamora. "Intentionally Equitable Hospitality as Critical Instructional Design," in Jerod Quinn and Martha Burtis, eds., *Designing for Care* (Hybrid Pedagogy, Inc., 2022). Accessed May 2, 2022. https://press-books.pub/designingforcare/chapter/intentionally-equitable-hospitality -as-critical-instructional-design/.

Bali, Maha, Autumm Caines, Rebecca J. Hogue, Helen J. DeWaard, and Christian Friedrich, "Intentionally Equitable Hospitality in Hybrid Video Dialogue: The Context of Virtually Connecting," *eLearn* 5, no. 5, May 2019. https://doi.org/10 .1145/3329488.3331173. https://elearnmag.acm.org/archive.cfm?aid=3331173.

Barton, Michelle A., Bill Kahn, Sally Maitlis, and Kathleen M. Sutcliffe. "Stop Fram-ing Wellness Programs around Self-Care," *Harvard Business Review*, April 4, 2022. https://hbr.org/2022/04/stop-framing-wellness-programs-around-self -care.

"Basic Needs Syllabus Integration." Open CoLab, Plymouth State University. Accessed May 1, 2023. https://colab.plymouthcreate.net/ace/ace-practice /basic-needs-and-gateless-policies-syllabus/.

Basso, Keith. *Wisdom Sits in Places: Landscape and Language among the Western Apache*. Albuquerque: University of New Mexico Press, 1996.

"Behavioral Health Equity." SAMHSA (Substance Abuse and Mental Health Services Administration). Updated May 25, 2023. https://www.samhsa.gov /behavioral-health-equity/resources.

Berntsen, Leslie. "How Not to Handle Student Failure." *Chronicle of Higher Education*, October 13, 2022. https://www.chronicle.com/article/how-not-to -handle-student-failure.

"The Big List of Self-Care Activities" (adapted from Matthew McKay, Jeffrey C. Wood, and Jeffrey Brantley, *The Dialectical Behavior Therapy Skills Workbook* [Oakland, CA: New Harbinger, 2007]). Indiana Youth Institute. Accessed May 2, 2023. https://www.iyi.org/wp-content/uploads/2020/02/Additional -Referenced-Resources.pdf.

Birt, Jamie. "14 Ways to Practice Self-Care at Work (and Why It Matters)." Indeed. Updated August 31, 2023. https://www.indeed.com/career-advice/career -development/selfcare-at-work.

Bliss, Eula. "The Landlord's Game: Eula Bliss on the Anticapitalist Origins of Monopoly," Literary Hub, September 2, 2020. https://lithub.com/the -landlords-game-eula-biss-on-the-anticapitalist-origins-of-monopoly/.

Blum, Susan D., ed. *Ungrading: Why Rating Students Undermines Learning (and What to Do Instead)*. Morgantown: West Virginia University Press, 2020.

Boring, Anne, and Arnaud Philippe. "Reducing Discrimination in the Field: Evi-dence from an Awareness-Raising Intervention Targeting Gender Biases in

Student Evaluations of Teaching." *Journal of Public Economics* 193 (January 2021): 104323. https://doi.org/10.1016/j.jpubeco.2020.104323.

Bowers, Mark, Patricia Fernandez, Megha Shah, Katherine Slager, Kelly Crecco, and Susanna Wagar. *Solitary Confinement as Torture.* University of North Car olina School of Law Immigration/Human Rights Clinic, 2014. https://law.unc .edu/wp-content/uploads/2019/10/solitaryconfinementreport.pdf.

Brach, Tara. *Radical Acceptance: Embracing Your Life with the Heart of a Buddha.* New York: Random House, 2004.

Brame, Cynthia J., and Rachel Biel. "Group Work: Using Cooperative Learning Groups Effectively." Center for Teaching, Vanderbilt University, 2015. https:// cft.vanderbilt.edu/guides-sub-pages/setting-up-and-facilitating-group-work -using-cooperative-learning-groups-effectively/.

Bringing History Home. "The Bringing History Home Evaluations." Accessed May 4, 2023. http://www.bringinghistoryhome.org/evaluations.

Brooks, René. "How to Guard Your Yes (and Figure Out When You Haven't Been Doing It!)," *Black Girl, Lost Keys* (blog), April 13, 2020. https://blackgirllostkeys .com/adhd/how-to-guard-your-yes/.

brown, adrienne maree. *Emergent Strategy: Shaping Change, Changing Worlds.* Chico, CA: AK Press, 2017.

Bruff, Derek. "In Defense of Continuous Exposition by the Teacher," *Agile Learning* (blog), September 15, 2015. https://derekbruff.org/?p=3126.

Brulliard, Karin. "Social Distancing Is So Hard because It's Contrary to Human Nature." *Washington Post*, March 17, 2020. https://www.washingtonpost.com /science/2020/03/17/coronavirus-social-distancing/.

Bücele, Stefan. "Evaluating the Link between Attendance and Performance in Higher Education: The Role of Classroom Engagement Dimensions," *Assessment and Evaluation in Higher Education* 46, no. 1 (2021): 132–50.

Buchanan, Thomas, and Edward Palmer, "Student Perceptions of the History Lecture: Does This Delivery Mode Have a Future in the Humanities?" *Journal of University Learning & Teaching Practice* 14, no. 2 (2017). https://doi.org /10.53761/1.14.2.4. https://ro.uow.edu.au/cgi/viewcontent.cgi?article=1701& context=jutlp.

Burgason, Kyle A., Ophir Sefiha, and Lisa Briggs. "Cheating Is in the Eye of the Beholder: An Evolving Understanding of Academic Misconduct." *Innovative Higher Education* 44, no. 3 (June 2019): 203–18. https://doi.org/10.1007 /s10755-019-9457-3.

Burgstahler, Sheryl E., ed., *Universal Design in Higher Education: From Principles to Practice.* Cambridge, MA: Harvard University Press, 2015.

Burkeman, Oliver. *Four Thousand Weeks: Time Management for Mortals.* New York: Farrar, Straus and Giroux, 2021.

Bursztynsky, Jessica. "UI Professor Leaves after Email Scandal Refusing to Accommodate Student," *Daily Illini*, September 12, 2017. https://dailyillini

.com/news-stories/campus-life/2017/09/12/ui-professor-leaves-refusing
-accommodate-student/.

Carruthers, Mary. *The Book of Memory: A Study of Memory in Medieval Culture.* 2nd ed. Cambridge: Cambridge University Press, 2008.

Cavanagh, Sarah Rose. *The Spark of Learning: Energizing the College Classroom with the Science of Emotion.* Teaching and Learning in Higher Education series. Morgantown: West Virginia University Press, 2016.

"Chart a Course: Ungrading with Courtney Sobers." Rutgers School of Arts & Sciences–Newark, YouTube, 2021. https://www.youtube.com/watch?v= YadoqOs6UpA.

Chick, Nancy. "Metacognition," Vanderbilt University Center for Teaching, 2013. https://cft.vanderbilt.edu/guides-sub-pages/metacognition/.

Chronis-Tuscano, Andrea. "ADHD in Girls and Women: A Call to Action— Reflections on Hinshaw et al. (2021)." *Journal of Child Psychology and Psychiatry.* 63, no, 4 (2022): 497–99. https://doi.org/10.1111/jcpp.13574.

Chödrön, Pema. *When Things Fall Apart: Heart Advice for Difficult Times.* Boston: Shambala, 2000.

Cohan, Deborah J. "Upholding Rigor at Pandemic U." Inside Higher Ed, August 24, 2021. https://www.insidehighered.com/advice/2021/08/25/professors-should -uphold-rigor-when-assessing-students-even-pandemic-opinion.

"Color Blindness." National Eye Institute. Updated August 11, 2013. https:// www.nei.nih.gov/learn-about-eye-health/eye-conditions-and-diseases/color -blindness.

"Coloring Pages for Adults," Just Color, copyright 2023. https://www.justcolor.net/.

Conrad, Rita Marie. "Taking Attendance: Must We?" Berkeley Center for Teaching and Learning. Accessed May 1, 2022. No longer online.

Cooper, Katelyn M., Brian Haney, Anna Krieg, and Sara E. Brownwell, "What's in a Name? The Importance of Students Perceiving That an Instructor Knows Their Names in a High-Enrollment Biology Classroom." *CBE—Life Sciences Education* 16, no. 1 (Spring 2017): 1–13. https://doi.org/10.1187/cbe.16-08-0265.

Costa, Karen Ray. "The Desire Path of Empty Classrooms." Medium, December 1, 2022. https://karenraycosta.medium.com/the-desire-path-of-empty -classrooms-72d7cc9f103d.

———. "Systems Aren't Scary." Medium, October 31, 2022. https://karenraycosta .medium.com/systems-arent-scary-e55d8ac63bc7.

———. "Trauma Aware Pedagogy." *Tea for Teaching* (podcast), June 8, 2022. https://teaforteaching.com/243-trauma-aware-pedagogy/.

Cozolino, Louis. "Nine Things Educators Need to Know about the Brain." Greater Good Magazine, March 19, 2013. https://greatergood.berkeley.edu /article/item/%20nine_things_educators_need_to_know_about_the_brain.

"Creating a Culture of Self-Care in the Workplace," Calm. Accessed April 29, 2023. https://business.calm.com/resources/blog/creating-a-culture-of-self-care-in -the-workplace.

currie, sarah madoka. "the mad manifesto," Ph.D. diss., University of Waterloo, 2023, 245. https://uwspace.uwaterloo.ca/bitstream/handle/10012/19689/Currie_Sarah.pdf?sequence=3&isAllowed=y.

currie, sarah madoka, and the students of W2022 ENGL 109-007, "beyond the community tradition: conjuring community-first syllabi in apocalypse time," Spark: A 4C4Equality Journal 4 (April 19, 2022). https://sparkactivism.com/beyond-the-ability-tradition/.

Curtice, Kaitlin. "What Do We Do When Our Favorite Leaders Leave Social Media Behind?" *Liminality Journal* (blog), June 23, 2022. https://kaitlincurtice.substack.com/p/what-do-we-do-when-our-favorite-leaders.

Dalai Lama. *My Land and My People: The Original Autobiography of His Holiness the Dalai Lama of Tibet.* New York: Warner Books, 1997.

———. *The Universe in a Single Atom: The Convergence of Science and Spirituality.* New York: Morgan Road Books, 2005.

Dancy, T. Elon, Kirsten T. Edwards, and James Earl Davis. "Historically White Universities and Plantation Politics: Anti-Blackness and Higher Education in the Black Lives Matter Era." *Urban Education* 53, no. 2 (2018): 176–95. https://doi.org/10.1177/0042085918754328.

Davis, Lennard J. "Where's the Outrage When Colleges Discriminate against Students with Disabilities?" *Chronicle of Higher Education*, July 23, 2015. https://www.chronicle.com/article/wheres-the-outrage-when-colleges-discriminate-against-students-with-disabilities/.

Denial, Cate. *Cate Denial* (blog). https://catherinedenial.org.

Denial, Cate, Clarissa Sorensen-Unruh, and Elizabeth Lehfeldt. "After the Great Pivot Should Come the Great Pause." *Chronicle of Higher Education*, February 25, 2022. https://www.chronicle.com/article/after-the-great-pivot-should-come-the-great-pause.

Denial, Catherine J. "Atoms, Honeycombs, and Fabric Scraps: Rethinking Timelines in the Undergraduate Classroom." *History Teacher* 46, no. 3 (May 2013): 415–34. https://www.jstor.org/stable/43264133.

Dolmage, Jay. "Universal Design: Places to Start." *Disability Studies Quarterly* 35, no. 2 (2015). https://dsq-sds.org/article/view/4632/3946.

Durm, Mark W. "An A Is Not an A: A History of Grading." *Educational Forum* 57, no. 3 (September 1993), 294–97. https://doi.org/10.1080/00131729309335429.

Espinosa, Lorelle L., Jonathan M. Turk, Morgan Taylor, and Hollie M. Chessman. "Enrollment in Undergraduate Education." In *Race and Ethnicity in Higher Education: A Status Report*, 37–67. American Council on Education, 2019. https://www.equityinhighered.org/resources/report-downloads/race-and-ethnicity-in-higher-education-a-status-report/.

"Everything Is Awful and I'm Not Okay: Questions to Ask before Giving Up." University of Washington Department of Family Medicine. Accessed May 2, 2023. https://depts.washington.edu/fammed/wp-content/uploads/2019/03/Katers-selfcare_printable.pdf.

Eyler, Joshua R. *Humans Learn: The Science and Stories behind Effective College Teaching*. Teaching and Learning in Higher Education series. Morgantown: West Virginia University Press, 2018.

Fasheh, Munir. "The Trouble with Knowledge." Shikshantar: The People's Institute for Rethinking Education and Development. Accessed May 2, 2023. https://shikshantar.org/articles/trouble-knowledge.

Flaherty, Colleen. "Death Knell for Trigger Warnings?" Inside Higher Ed, March 21, 2019. https://www.insidehighered.com/news/2019/03/21/new-study-says-trigger-warnings-are-useless-does-mean-they-should-be-abandoned.

———. "What Students Want (and Don't) from Their Professors." Inside Higher Ed, March 24, 2023. https://www.insidehighered.com/news/2023/03/24/survey-faculty-teaching-style-impedes-academic-success-students-say.

Freeman, Scott, Sarah L. Eddy, Miles McDonough, Michelle K. Smith, Nnadozie Okoroafor, Hannah Jordt, and Mary Pat Wenderoth. "Active Learning Increases Student Performance in Science, Engineering, and Mathematics." *Proceedings of the National Academy of Sciences* 111, no. 23 (June 2014): 8410–15. https://doi.org/10.1073/pnas.1319030111.

Frisby, Brandi N., and Matthew M. Martin. "Instructor-Student and Student-Student Rapport in the Classroom." *Communication Education* 59, no. 2 (April 2010), 146–64. https://doi.org/10.1080/03634520903564362.

Freire, Paulo. *Pedagogy of the Oppressed: 50th Anniversary Edition*. New York: Bloomsbury, 2018.

Frye, Devon. "The Children Left Behind." *ADDitude*, March 31, 2022. https://www.additudemag.com/race-and-adhd-how-people-of-color-get-left-behind/.

Galanes, Philip. "Is Extra Help Hurting My Friend with Autism?" *New York Times*, April 19, 2018. https://www.nytimes.com/2018/04/19/style/is-extra-help-hurting-my-friend-with-autism.html.

Gannon, Kevin. "How to Create a Syllabus: Advice Guide." *Chronicle of Higher Education*. Accessed May 1, 2023. https://www.chronicle.com/article/how-to-create-a-syllabus/.

Gannon, Kevin M. *Radical Hope: A Teaching Manifesto*. Teaching and Learning in Higher Education. Morgantown: West Virginia University Press, 2020.

Geiger, Roger L. *The History of American Higher Education: Learning and Culture from the Founding to World War II*. Princeton, NJ: Princeton University Press, 2016.

Geng, Lucia. "Mutual Aid Goes Mainstream." *Dissent*, Fall 2021. https://www.dissentmagazine.org/article/mutual-aid-goes-mainstream.

Glazier, Rebecca A., Tobias Wilson-Bates, Kristin Croyle, Emily Isaacs, Elaine M. Hernandez, and Nicole Green. "How to Solve the Student Disengagement Crisis: Six Experts Diagnose the Problem—and Suggest Ways to Fix It." *Chronicle of Higher Education*, May 11, 2022. https://www.chronicle.com/article/how-to-solve-the-student-disengagement-crisis.

Godbee, Beth. "Beth Godbee, Ph.D." Head-Heart-Hands.com, July 12, 2019. https://heart-head-hands.com/beth-godbee/.

Goldrick-Rab, Sara. "Basic Needs Security and the Syllabus." Medium, August 7, 2017. https://saragoldrickrab.medium.com/basic-needs-security-and-the -syllabus-d24cc7afe8c9.

"Graduate Student Emergency Support Fund." University of Notre Dame, Graduate School. Accessed April 29, 2023. https://graduateschool.nd.edu/policies -forms/graduate-student-assistance/graduate-student-emergency-support -fund/.

Grasgreen, Allie. "Dropping the Ball on Disabilities." Inside Higher Ed, April 2, 2014. https://www.insidehighered.com/news/2014/04/02/students-disabilities -frustrated-ignorance-and-lack-services.

Gray, Brenna Clarke. "Five Conversations about Education I Would Rather Eat Glass Than Continue Having." *Little EdTech, Big Mouth* (blog), November 10, 2022. https://blog.brennaclarkegray.ca/2022/11/10/five-conversations-about -education-i-would-rather-eat-glass-than-continue-having/.

Haimson, Olive L., and Lee Airton, "Making Space for Them, Her, Him, and 'Prefer Not to Disclose' in Group Settings: Why Pronoun-Sharing Is Important but Must Remain Optional." National Center for Institutional Diversity, June 4, 2019. https://medium.com/national-center-for-institutional-diversity /making-space-for-them-her-him-and-prefer-not-to-disclose-in-group -settings-why-1deb8c3d6b86.

Haines, Staci K. *The Politics of Trauma: Somatics, Healing, and Social Justice.* Berkeley, CA: North Atlantic Books, 2019.

Hanson, Aubrey Jean. *Literatures, Communities, and Learning: Conversations with Indigenous Writers.* Indigenous Studies Series. Waterloo, ON: Wilfred Laurier University Press, 2020.

Harrington, Christine M., and Crystal A. Gabert-Quillen. "Syllabus Length and Use of Images: An Empirical Investigation of Student Perceptions." *Scholarship of Teaching and Learning in Psychology* 1, no. 3 (2015): 235–43. https://doi .org/10.1037/stl0000040.

Hartocollis, Anemona. "A Lawsuit Accuses Harvard of Ignoring Sexual Harassment by a Professor." *New York Times*, February 8, 2022. https://www.nytimes .com/2022/02/08/us/harvard-sexual-harassment-lawsuit.html.

Herrman, John. "The Buy-Nothing Home Office." *New York Times*, April 15, 2020. https://www.nytimes.com/2020/04/15/style/working-from-home-setup.html.

Hernandez, Joe. "1 in 4 American Jews Say They Experienced Anti-Semitism in the Last Year," NPR, October 26, 2021. https://www.npr.org/2021/10/26 /1049288223/1-in-4-american-jews-say-they-experienced-antisemitism-in -the-last-year.

Hinshaw, Stephen P., Phuc T. Nguyen, Sinclaire M. O'Grady, and Emily A. Rosenthal. "Annual Research Review: Attention-Deficit/Hyperactivity Disorder in

Girls and Women: Underrepresentation, Longitudinal Processes, and Key Directions." *Journal of Child Psychology and Psychiatry* 63, no. 4 (April 2022): 484–96. https://doi.org/10.1111/jcpp.13480.

Hogan, Kelly A., and Viji Sathy. *Inclusive Teaching: Strategies for Promoting Equity in the College Classroom*. Teaching and Learning in Higher Education series. Morgantown: West Virginia University Press, 2022.

Hollis, James. *What Matters Most: Living a More Considered Life*. New York: Gotham Books, 2009.

hooks, bell. *Teaching to Transgress: Education as the Practice of Freedom*. New York: Routledge, 1994.

The Hope Center Survey 2021: Basic Needs Insecurity in the Ongoing Pandemic. Hope Center for College, Community, and Justice, Temple University, March 31, 2021. https://hope.temple.edu/sites/hope/files/media/document/HopeSurveyReport2021.pdf.

"How to Create and Manage Groups." Center for Teaching Innovation, Cornell University. Accessed May 2, 2023. https://teaching.cornell.edu/teaching-resources/active-collaborative-learning/how-create-and-manage-groups.

"IGR Insight Handouts." Program on Intergroup Relations, University of Michigan. Accessed May 2, 2023. https://igr.umich.edu/IGR-Insight-Handouts.

Immordino-Yang, Mary Helen. *Emotions, Learning, and the Brain: Exploring the Educational Implications of Affective Neuroscience*. New York: W. W. Norton, 2016.

"Introductory Activities: Creative Ways to Do Student Introductions on Your First Week of Classes." OneHE. Accessed May 2, 2022. https://onehe.org/equity-unbound/introductory-activities/.

Isbister, Katherine. "Fidget Toys Aren't Just Hype," *The Conversation*, May 17, 2017. https://theconversation.com/fidget-toys-arent-just-hype-77456.

Jack, Jordynn, and Viji Sathy. "It's Time to Cancel the Word Rigor." *Chronicle of Higher Education*, September 24, 2021. https://www.chronicle.com/article/its-time-to-cancel-the-word-rigor.

Jenkins, Bailey D., Jonathan M. Golding, Alexis M. Le Grand, Mary M. Levi, and Andrea M. Pals. "When Opportunity Knocks: College Students' Cheating amid the COVID-19 Pandemic." *Teaching of Psychology* 50, no. 4 (2023): 407–19. https://doi.org/10.1177/00986283211059067.

Joseph, A. Skylar. "A Modern Trail of Tears: The Missing and Murdered Indigenous Women (MMIW) Crisis in the U.S." *Journal of Forensic and Legal Medicine* 79 (April 2021): 102136. https://doi.org/10.1016/j.jflm.2021.102136.

Justice, Nicola. "Preparing Graduate Students to Teach Statistics: A Review of Research and Ten Practical Recommendations." *Journal of Statistics Education* 28, no. 3 (2020): 334–43. https://www.tandfonline.com/doi/full/10.1080/10691898.2020.1841590/.

Kalir, Remi. "Annotate Your Syllabus, 4.0." *Remi Kalir: remi(x)learning* (blog), August 8, 2022. https://remikalir.com/blog/annotate-your-syllabus-4-0/.

Kamenetz, Roger. *The Jew in the Lotus: A Poet's Rediscovery of Jewish Identity in Buddhist India*. New York: HarperOne, 2007.

Kang, Rachel. "The Journey to Accessible Apps." *Xamarin* (Microsoft Developer blog), April 14, 2021. https://devblogs.microsoft.com/xamarin/the-journey-to-accessible-apps/.

Keegin, Joseph M. "The Hysterical Style in the American Humanities: On the Ideological Posturing and Moral Nitpicking of the Very Online." *Chronicle of Higher Education*, June 15, 2022. https://www.chronicle.com/article/the-hysterical-style-in-the-american-humanities.

Kennedy, Robert F. "Day of Affirmation Address, University of Cape Town, Cape Town, South Africa, June 6, 1966." John F. Kennedy Presidential Library and Museum. Accessed May 2, 2023. https://www.jfklibrary.org/learn/about-jfk/the-kennedy-family/robert-f-kennedy/robert-f-kennedy-speeches/day-of-affirmation-address-university-of-capetown-capetown-south-africa-june-6-1966.

Keown, Damien. *Buddhism: A Very Short Introduction*. New York: Oxford University Press, 2013.

Khalid, Amna, and Jeffrey Aaron Snyder. "The Data Is In—Trigger Warnings Don't Work." *Chronicle of Higher Education*, September 15, 2021. https://www.chronicle.com/article/the-data-is-in-trigger-warnings-dont-work.

King, Jina B., and Sami Schalk. "Reclaiming the Radical Politics of Self-Care: A Crip-of-Color Critique." *South Atlantic Quarterly* 120, no. 2 (April 2021): 325–42. https://doi.org/10.1215/00382876-8916074.

Kodipady, Aditi, Gordon Kraft-Todd, Gregg Sparkman, Blair Hu, and Liane Young. "Beyond Virtue Signaling: Perceived Motivations for Pronoun Sharing." *Journal of Applied Social Psychology* (October 2022): 1–18. https://doi.org/10.1111/jasp.12937.

Kohn, Alfie. "The Case against Grades." Alfie Kohn, November 2011. https://www.alfiekohn.org/article/case-grades/.

Lammers, William J., and J. Arthur Gillaspy Jr. "Brief Measure of Student-Instructor Rapport Predicts Student Success in Online Courses." *International Journal for the Scholarship of Teaching and Learning* 7, no. 2 (July 2013), article 16. https://doi.org/10.20429/ijsotl.2013.070216.

Lau, Travis Chi Wing. "Slowness, Disability, and Academic Productivity: The Need to Rethink Academic Culture." In *Disability and the University: A Disabled Students' Manifesto*, ed. Christopher McMaster and Benjamin Whitburn, 11–19. New York: Peter Lang, 2019.

Levin, Rachel N. "The Problem with Pronouns." Inside Higher Ed, September 18, 2018. https://www.insidehighered.com/views/2018/09/19/why-asking-students-their-preferred-pronoun-not-good-idea-opinion.

"Lifestyle Spending Account." Ohio State University. Accessed April 29, 2023. https://hr.osu.edu/benefits/lsa/.

Liu, Jennifer. "When Work and Home Are the Same Place, Experts Say This Is How to Find Balance." CNBC, March 27, 2020. https://www.cnbc.com/2020/03/27/when-work-and-home-are-the-same-place-this-is-how-to-find-balance.html.

Lorde, Audre. *A Burst of Light and Other Essays.* 1988. Reprint, New York: Ixia Press, 2017.

Love, Bettina L. *We Want to Do More Than Survive: Abolitionist Teaching and the Pursuit of Educational Freedom.* Boston: Beacon Press, 2019.

———. "White Teachers Need Anti-Racist Therapy." *Education Week*, February 6, 2020. https://www.edweek.org/ew/articles/2020/02/07/all-teachers-need-therapy-white-teachers-need.html.

MacDonald, Kris. "A Review of the Literature: The Needs of Non-Traditional Students in Post-Secondary Education." *Strategic Enrollment Management Quarterly* 5, no. 4 (January 2018): 159–64. https://doi.org/10.1002/sem3.20115.

MacNell, Lillian, Adam Driscoll, and Andrea N. Hunt. "What's in a Name? Exposing Gender Bias in Student Ratings of Teaching." *Innovative Higher Education* 40 (2015): 291–303. https://doi.org/10.1007/s10755-014-9313-4.

"Managing Difficult Classroom Conversations." Center for Innovative Teaching and Learning, Indiana University Bloomington. Accessed May 2, 2023. https://citl.indiana.edu/teaching-resources/diversity-inclusion/managing-difficult-classroom-discussions/index.html.

Marama, Yamiko. "Reading Audre Lorde in the Age of #Self-Care." Kill Your Darlings, June 3, 2021. https://www.killyourdarlings.com.au/article/rereading-audre-lorde-in-the-age-of-self-care/.

Marcus, Ezra. "How College Students Are Helping Each Other Survive." *New York Times*, November 23, 2020. https://www.nytimes.com/2020/11/23/style/college-mutual-aid-networks.html.

Marshall, Kelli. "Why I Don't Take Attendance." *Chronicle of Higher Education*, October 12, 2017. https://www.chronicle.com/article/why-i-dont-take-attendance/.

Masland, Lindsay C. "Ungrading: The Joys of Doing Everything Wrong." *Zeal: A Journal for the Liberal Arts* 1, no. 2 (2023): 88–93. https://zeal.kings.edu/zeal/article/view/23.

Mazzula, Silvia Lorena. "Wholeness and Hope in Education: This Is What a Professor Looks Like." *Psych Learning Curve.* May 7, 2018. http://psychlearningcurve.org/wholeness-and-hope-in-education-this-is-what-a-professor-looks-like/.

McCloud, Laila I. "Keeping Receipts: Thoughts on Ungrading from a Black Woman Professor." *Zeal: A Journal for the Liberal Arts* 1, no. 2 (April 2023): 101–5. https://zeal.kings.edu/zeal/article/view/25.

McCoy, Henrika. "What Do You Call a Black Woman with a PhD? A N*****: How Race Trumps Education No Matter What." *Race and Justice* 11, no. 3 (2021): 318–27. https://doi.org/10.1177/2153368720988892.

McCoy, James P., and Martin I. Milkman. "Do Recent PhD Economists Feel Prepared to Teach Economics?" *Journal of Economic Education*, 41, no. 2 (April–June 2010): 211–15. https://www.jstor.org/stable/25766054.

McDaniel, Caleb. "Generic Syllabus Maker," Rice University. Accessed May 1, 2023. http://wcaleb.rice.edu/syllabusmaker/generic/.

McMurtrie, Beth. "A 'Stunning' Level of Student Disconnection." *Chronicle of Higher Education*, April 5, 2022. https://www.chronicle.com/article/a-stunning-level-of-student-disconnection.

Miceli, Heather. "Ungrading in a General Education Science Course," June 11, 2021. In *Crowdsourcing Ungrading*, convened by David Buck. Pressbooks, 2020. https://pressbooks.howardcc.edu/ungrading/chapter/ungrading-in-a-general-education-science-course/.

Miller, Angela D., Tamera B. Murdock, and Morgan M. Grotewiel. "Addressing Academic Dishonesty among the Highest Achievers." *Theory into Practice* 56, no. 2 (2017): 121–28. https://doi.org/10.1080/00405841.2017.1283574.

Miller, Greg. "Social Distancing Prevents Infections, but It Can Have Unintended Consequences." *Science*. March 16, 2020. https://www.science.org/content/article/we-are-social-species-how-will-social-distancing-affect-us.

Mintz, Steven. "An Epidemic of Student Disengagement: Eight Ways to Re-Engage Disconnected College Students." Inside Higher Ed, April 13, 2022. https://www.insidehighered.com/blogs/higher-ed-gamma/epidemic-student-disengagement.

Morgan, Paul L., Jeremy Staff, Marianne M. Hillemeier, George Farkas, and Steven Maczuga. "Racial and Ethnic Disparities in ADHD Diagnosis from Kindergarten to Eighth Grade." *Pediatrics* 132, no. 1 (July 2013): 85–93. https://doi.org/10.1542/peds.2012-2390.

Mowreader, Ashley. "Academic Success Tip: Help Students Excel at Organization." Inside Higher Ed, March 16, 2023. https://www.insidehighered.com/news/2023/03/17/academic-coaches-organize-student-deadlines.

Mwangi, Chrystal A. George, Barbara Thelamour, Ijeoma Ezeofor, and Ashley Carpenter. "'Black Elephant in the Room': Black Students Contextualizing Campus Racial Climate within U.S. Racial Climate." *Journal of College Student Development* 59, no. 4 (July–August 2018): 456–74. https://doi.org/10.1353/csd.2018.0042. https://scholarworks.umass.edu/cgi/viewcontent.cgi?article=1027&context=cfssr_publishedwork.

National College Health Assessment II: Undergraduate Student Reference Group, Executive Summary, Spring 2019. American College Health Association, 2019. https://www.acha.org/documents/ncha/NCHA-II_SPRING_2019_UNDERGRADUATE_REFERENCE%20_GROUP_EXECUTIVE_SUMMARY.pdf.

Nave, Lillian. *Think UDL* (podcast), various dates. Accessed May 1, 2023. https://thinkudl.org/.

"Navigating Difficult Moments." Derek Bok Center for Teaching and Learning, Harvard University. Accessed May 2, 2023. https://bokcenter.harvard.edu /navigating-difficult-moments.

Neuhaus, Jessamyn, ed., *Geeky Pedagogy: A Guide for Intellectuals, Introverts, and Nerds Who Want to Be Effective Teachers.* Teaching and Learning in Higher Education. Morgantown: West Virginia University Press, 2019.

———. *Picture a Professor: Interrupting Biases about Faculty and Increasing Student Learning.* Teaching and Learning in Higher Education series. Morgantown: West Virginia University Press, 2022.

"New Wellness Benefits Available to Eligible Faculty and Staff," Ohio State University, January 26, 2023. https://hr.osu.edu/news/2023/01/26/new-wellness -benefits-available-for-eligible-faculty-and-staff/.

Noddings, Nel. *Caring: A Relational Approach to Ethics and Moral Education.* 2nd ed. Berkeley: University of California Press, 2013.

"Nontraditional Undergraduates: Trends in Enrollment from 1986 to 1992 and Persistence and Attainment among 1989–90 Beginning Postsecondary Students." National Center for Education Statistics, Statistical Analysis Report, November 1996. https://nces.ed.gov/pubs/97578.pdf.

Novikoff, Alex J. *The Medieval Culture of Disputation: Pedagogy, Practice, and Performance.* The Middle Ages series. Philadelphia: University of Pennsylvania Press, 2013.

"NWSA Statemen on Threats to the Field in Higher Education and Beyond." National Women's Studies Association, 2022. https://mailchi.mp/nwsa/nwsa -statement-on-threats-to-the-field-in-higher-education-and-beyond.

Nye, Naomi Shihab. "Kindness," 1995. https://poets.org/poem/kindness.

O'Brien, Molly Townes, Tania Leiman, and James Duffy, "The Power of Naming: The Multifaceted Value of Learning Students' Names." *QUT Law Review* 14, no. 1 (2014): 114–28. https://doi.org/10.5204/qutlr.v14i1.544.

Ocasio-Cortez, Alexandria, and Mariame Kaba, "Mutual Aid 101 Toolkit." Accessed April 29, 2023. https://cdn.cosmicjs.com/09a653b0-7545-11ea-be6b -9f10a20c6f68-Mutual-Aid-101-Toolkit.pdf.

O'Donnell, Daniel Paul. "The Unessay." *Daniel Paul O'Donnell* (blog), last modified September 28, 2018. https://people.uleth.ca/~daniel.odonnell/Teaching /the-unessay.

"Ohio 4-H Healthy Living Journal." Ohio State University. Accessed April 29, 2023. https://u.osu.edu/4hjournal/.

"On Learning Goals and Learning Objectives." Derek Bok Center for Teaching and Learning, Harvard University. Accessed May 1, 2023. https://bokcenter .harvard.edu/learning-goals-and-learning-objectives.

O'Reilley, Mary Rose. *The Barn at the End of the World: The Apprenticeship of a Quaker, Buddhist Shepherd.* Minneapolis: Milkweed Editions, 2001.

———. *Radical Presence: Teaching as Contemplative Practice.* Portsmouth, NH: Boynton/Cook Publishers, 1998.

Osborne, Natalie. "Intersectionality and Kyriarchy: A Framework for Approaching Power and Social Justice in Planning and Climate Change Adaptation." *Planning Theory* 14, no. 2 (2015): 130–51. https://doi.org/10.1177/1473095213 516443.

Pacansky-Brock, Michelle. "Humanizing Pre-Course Contact with a Liquid Syllabus." Brocansky.com, June 9, 2020. https://brocansky.com/2020/06/humanizing-pre-course-contact-with-a-liquid-syllabus.html.

———. "The Liquid Syllabus: An Anti-Racist Teaching Element." *C2C Digital Magazine*, Spring–Summer 2021. https://scalar.usc.edu/works/c2c-digital-magazine-spring--summer-2021/the-liquid-syllabus-anti-racist.

Perry, Armon R., Sherri L. Wallace, Sharon E. Moore, and Gwendolyn D. Perry-Burney. "Understanding Student Evaluations: A Black Faculty Perspective." *Reflections: Narratives of Professional Helping* 20, no. 1 (2015): 29–35.

Petersen, Anne Helen. The Case for Lunch." *Culture Study* (blog). June 19, 2022. https://annehelen.substack.com/p/the-case-for-lunch.

———. "So You've Decided to Bungle Your Company's Flexible Work Plan: The Four Most Popular Bungles and Four Very Straightforward Alternatives." *Culture Study* (blog), July 6, 2022. https://annehelen.substack.com/p/so-youve-decided-to-bungle-your-companys.

———. "Why Are Bosses So Miserable?" *Culture Study* (blog), October 20, 2022. https://annehelen.substack.com/p/why-are-bosses-so-miserable.

Piepzna-Samarasinha, Leah Lakshmi. *Care Work: Dreaming Disability Justice*. Vancouver, British Columbia: Arsenal Pulp Press, 2018.

Pinto, Jo Ann M., and Peter Lohrey. "Point-Counterpoint: Should Attendance Be Required in Collegiate Classrooms?" *Contemporary Issues in Education Research* 9, no. 3 (2016): 115–20. https://doi.org/10.19030/cier.v9i3.9706.

Plowe, Ed. "Don't Ask Me for My Pronouns Yet." *Cornell Daily Sun*, August 30, 2022. https://cornellsun.com/2022/08/30/plowe-dont-ask-me-for-my-pronouns-yet/.

Price, Devon. *Laziness Does Not Exist*. New York: Simon & Schuster, 2022.

———. "Laziness Does Not Exist." Medium, March 23, 2018. https://humanparts.medium.com/laziness-does-not-exist-3af27e312d01.

———. *Unmasking Autism: Discovering the New Faces of Neurodiversity*. New York: Harmony, 2022.

Price, Margaret. *Mad at School: Rhetorics of Mental Disability and Academic Life*. Ann Arbor: University of Michigan Press, 2011.

Pusateri, Jennifer L. *Transform Your Teaching with Universal Design: Six Steps to Jumpstart Your Practice*. Wakefield, MA: CAST, 2022.

Rasamny, Mia. "A Clear Violation of the Law." *Hoya*, February 4, 2022. https://thehoya.com/a-clear-violation-of-the-law-professors-reject-student-disability-accommodations/.

"Read Aloud: Voice Enabling the Web." Accessed May 7, 2023. https://readaloud.app/.

"Research: Our Findings on the Future of Work." Future Forum, Summer 2021–Winter 2023. https://futureforum.com/research/.

Responding to Triggers (video and transcript), excerpt from Community Organizing for Social Justice (course). Michigan Online. Accessed May 2, 2023. https://online.umich.edu/collections/racism-antiracism/short/responding-triggers/.

Ridder-Symoens, Hilde de, ed. *A History of the University in Europe*, 4 vols. Vol. 1: *Universities in the Middle Ages.* Cambridge: Cambridge University Press, 1991.

Robinson, Jennifer Meta, Valerie Dean O'Loughlin, Katherine D. Kearns, and Catherine Sherwood-Laughlin, "The Graduate Course in Pedagogy: Survey of Instructors of College Pedagogy in the United States and Canada," *College Teaching* 67, no. 2 (2019): 109–19. https://doi.org/10.1080/87567555.2018.1558171.

Robinson, Terrell E. and Warren C. Hope, "Teaching in Higher Education: Is There a Need for Training in Pedagogy in Graduate Degree Programs?" *Research in Higher Education Journal* 21 (August 2013). https://files.eric.ed.gov/fulltext/EJ1064657.pdf.

Rockquemore, Kerry Ann. "Call Me Doctor _____." Inside Higher Ed, March 11, 2015. https://www.insidehighered.com/advice/2015/03/11/advice-young-black-woman-academe-about-not-being-called-doctor.

Ruttenberg, Danya. *On Repentance and Repair: Making Amends in an Unapologetic World.* Boston: Beacon Press, 2022.

Samaran, Nora. *Turn the World Inside Out: The Emergence of Nurturance Culture.* Chico, CA: AK Press, 2019.

Sanson, Mevagh, Deryn Strange, and Maryanne Garry. "Trigger Warnings Are Trivially Helpful at Reducing Negative Affect, Intrusive Thoughts, and Avoidance." *Clinical Psychological Science* 7, no. 4 (July 2019): 778–93. https://doi.org/10.1177/2167702619827018.

Sathy, Viji, Kelly A. Hogan, and Bob Henshaw. "The More You Know about Your Students, the More Inclusive You Can Be in the Classroom." *Chronicle of Higher Education*, June 21, 2022. https://www.chronicle.com/article/the-more-you-know-about-your-students-the-more-inclusive-you-can-be-in-the-classroom.

Schinske, Jeffrey, and Kimberly Tanner, "Teaching by Grading Less (or Differently)," *CBE—Life Sciences Education* 13, no. 2 (Summer 2014): 159–66. https://doi.org/10.1187/cbe.cbe-14-03-0054.

Schoen, Johanna. *Choice and Coercion: Birth Control, Sterilization, and Abortion in Public Health and Welfare.* Gender and American Culture series. Chapel Hill: University of North Carolina Press, 2005.

"Self-Care Inventory" (adapted from Child Welfare Training Toolkit, March 2008; original source unknown). National Alliance on Mental Illness. Accessed May 2, 2023. https://www.nami.org/NAMI/media/Extranet-Education/HF15AR6SelfCare.pdf.

Sharpe, Christina. *In the Wake: On Blackness and Being.* Durham, NC: Duke University Press, 2016.

Shihipar, Abdullah. "These Students Took Care of Each Other When Their Universities Didn't," *The Nation,* April 13, 2020. https://www.thenation.com/article/society/these-students-took-care-of-each-other-when-their-universities-didnt/.

Spade, Dean. *Mutual Aid: Building Solidarity during This Crisis (and the Next).* London: Verso Books, 2020.

Smith, Linda Tuhiwai. *Decolonizing Methodologies: Research and Indigenous Peoples.* 2nd ed. London: Zed Books, 2012.

"Social Identity Wheel." LSA Inclusive Teaching, University of Michigan. Accessed April 29, 2023. https://sites.lsa.umich.edu/inclusive-teaching/social-identity-wheel/.

Sorber, Nathan M. *Land-Grant Colleges and Popular Revolt: The Origins of the Morrill Act and the Reform of Higher Education.* Ithaca, NY: Cornell University Press, 2018.

Stains, Robert R., Jr., and John Sarrouf. "Hard to Say; Hard to Hear; Heart to Heart: Inviting and Harnessing Strong Emotions in Dialogue for Deliberation." *Journal of Deliberative Democracy.* 18, no. 2 (2022): 1–5. https://doi.org/10.16997/jdd.979.

"Statement on Standards of Professional Conduct (Updated 2023)," American Historical Association. https://www.historians.org/jobs-and-professional-development/statements-standards-and-guidelines-of-the-discipline/statement-on-standards-of-professional-conduct.

Stephanie. "Ungrading: A Review, a Retrospective, a Messy Path Ahead." Michigan State University, College of Education, Digital Instruction Support Community. July 21, 2021. https://education.msu.edu/digital-instruction-support-community/uncategorized/ungrading-a-review-a-retrospective-a-messy-path-ahead/.

Stommel, Jesse. "How to Ungrade." Jesse Stommel, March 11, 2018. https://www.jessestommel.com/how-to-ungrade/.

"Students with Disabilities." National Center for Education Statistics. Accessed April 20, 2023. https://nces.ed.gov/fastfacts/display.asp?id=60.

Su, Amy Jen. "Six Ways to Weave Self-Care into Your Workday." *Harvard Business Review.* June 19, 2017. https://hbr.org/2017/06/6-ways-to-weave-self-care-into-your-workday.

Supiano, Beckie. "The Unintended Consequences of 'Ungrading': Does Getting Rid of Grades Make Things Worse for Disadvantaged Students?" *Chronicle of Higher Education,* April 29, 2022. https://www.chronicle.com/article/the-unintended-consequences-of-ungrading.

Swindle, Jean, and Larissa Malone. "Testimonials of Exodus: Self-Emancipation in Higher Education through the Power of Womanism." In *We're Not OK: Black Faculty Experiences and Higher Education Strategies,* ed. Antija M. Allen and Justin T. Stewart, 147–68. Cambridge: Cambridge University Press, 2022.

Syphers, David. "In Defense of Rigor," *Inside Higher Ed*, September 22, 2021. https://www.insidehighered.com/views/2021/09/22/why-rigor-instruction -matters.

Thelin, John R. *A History of American Higher Education*, 3rd ed. Baltimore: Johns Hopkins University Press, 2019.

"'They Treat You Like You Are Worthless': Internal DHS Reports of Abuses by U.S. Border Officials." Human Rights Watch, October 21, 2021. https://www .hrw.org/report/2021/10/21/they-treat-you-you-are-worthless/internal-dhs -reports-abuses-us-border-officials#.

Thompson, Phyllis, and Janice Carello, eds. *Trauma-Informed Pedagogies: A Guide for Responding to Crisis and Inequality in Higher Education*. New York: Palgrave Macmillan, 2022.

"TILT Higher Ed Examples and Resources." TILT Higher Ed. Accessed May 2, 2023. https://tilthighered.com/tiltexamplesandresources.

"Tips for Learning Student Names." Teaching and Learning Resource Center, Ohio State University. Accessed May 2, 2023. https://teaching.resources.osu .edu/examples/tips-learning-student-names.

Tobin, Thomas J., and Kirsten T. Behling. *Reach Everyone, Teach Everyone: Universal Design for Learning in Higher Education*. Teaching and Learning in Higher Education series. Morgantown: West Virginia University Press, 2018.

Tomasello, Michael. "The Ultra-Social Animal." *European Journal of Social Psychology* 44, no. 3 (April 2014): 187–94. https://doi.org/10.1002%2Fejsp.2015.

"The UDL Guidelines." CAST. Accessed May 1, 2023. https://udlguidelines.cast .org/.

"United Way Compassion Fund." University of Notre Dame. Accessed April 29, 2023. https://unitedway.nd.edu/compassion-fund/.

Vansina, Jan. *Paths in the Rainforest: Toward a History of Political Tradition in Equatorial Africa*. Madison: University of Wisconsin Press, 1990.

Venet, Alex Shevrin. *Equity-Centered Trauma-Informed Education*. New York: W. W. Norton, 2021.

Volpe, Allie. "Why Community Matters So Much—and How to Find Yours," Vox, March 24, 2022. https://www.vox.com/22992901/how-to-find-your -community-as-an-adult.

Waziyatawin, Ph.D. *What Does Justice Look Like? The Struggle for Liberation in Dakota Homeland*. St. Paul, MN: Living Justice Press, 2008.

Waziyatawin Angela Wilson. *Remember This! Dakota Decolonization and the Eli Taylor Narratives*. Contemporary Indigenous Issues series. Lincoln: University of Nebraska Press, 2005.

Webb, Nathan G., and Laura Obrycki Barrett. "Student Views of Instructor-Student Rapport in the College Classroom." *Journal of the Scholarship of Teaching and Learning* 14, no. 2 (2014): 15–28. https://doi.org/10.14434/josotl.v14i2 .4259.

"What Are Best Practices for Designing Group Projects?" Eberly Center, Carnegie Mellon University. Accessed May 2, 2023. https://www.cmu.edu/teaching /designteach/teach/instructionalstrategies/groupprojects/design.html.

White, Luise. *Speaking with Vampires: Rumor and History in Colonial Africa.* Studies on the History of Society and Culture series. Oakland: University of California Press, 2000.

White, Luise, Stephan F. Miescher, and David William Cohen, eds. *African Words, African Voices: Critical Practices in Oral History.* Bloomington: Indiana University Press, 2001.

Wise, Sonny Jane. "Neurodivergent Umbrella," Instagram, December 28, 2021. https://www.instagram.com/p/CYBl-miPcCL/?hl=en.

Wiggins, Grant, and Jay McTighe. *Understanding by Design,* 2nd ed. Alexandria, VA: Association for Supervision and Curriculum Development, 2005.

Wilder, Craig Steven. *Ebony and Ivory: Race, Slavery, and the Troubled History of America's Universities.* New York: Bloomsbury, 2014.

Wilson, Shawn. *Research Is Ceremony: Indigenous Research Methods.* Halifax, NS: Fernwood Publishing, 2008.

Win, Em. "How to Host a Restorative Dinner Party for Your Chosen Queer Fam." Autostraddle, June 14, 2022. https://www.autostraddle.com/how-to -host-a-restorative-dinner-party-for-your-chosen-queer-fam/?utm_source= pocket_mylist.

Worthen, Molly. "Lecture Me. Really." *New York Times.* October 17, 2015. https:// www.nytimes.com/2015/10/18/opinion/sunday/lecture-me-really.html.

Young, Simon N. "The Neurobiology of Human Social Behaviour: An Important but Neglected Topic." *Journal of Psychiatry and Neuroscience* 33, no. 5 (2008): 391–92. https://www.ncbi.nlm.nih.gov/pmc/articles/PMC2527715/.

"Bread and Roses." Zinn Education Project. Reprinted from Labor Notes 2007. https://www.zinnedproject.org/materials/bread-and-roses-song/.

Zúñiga, Ximena. "Bridging Differences through Dialogue." *About Campus* 7, no. 6 (2003): 8–16. https://doi.org/10.1177/108648220300700603.

INDEX

Abdullah, Shaima, 97
ableism: academia and, 1, 9, 102;
  accommodations and, 65–68;
  assessment and, 63–65; disability
  as part of self, 7
academia: as ableist, 64;
  communication and expectation
  in, 61; isolation and, 33; need for
  kindness in, 101–4; representation
  and, 48; self-care and, 17–18;
  shortcomings of, 1–2
accessibility: classrooms and, 103;
  syllabi and, 52–55, 59; unessay
  projects and, 70; Universal Design
  for Learning and, 66–68
accommodations, 65–68, 89, 103
accountability, 18, 39, 100, 102
Anderson, Jenny, 34
Armon, Mary, 77–78
assessment activities: ableism and,
  63–65; affirming importance of,
  79; COVID-19 pandemic and,
  62–63, 77; expectations and, 59–61;
  feedback and, 74–76; grading and,
  71–73, 120n25; "hidden curriculum"
  and, 62–63; ink color and, 121n32;
  learning curves and, 120n18;
  participation and, 93; reevaluation
  of, 68–69, 80; rigor and, 62–63;
  structure and accessibility in, 80;
  student expression of knowledge
  and, 61, 68–69, 94; student
  input and, 74, 76; student self-
  reflection and, 75–76; transparent
  assignment design and, 77–79;

unessay projects and, 69–71;
  ungrading and, 73–74; Universal
  Design for Learning and, 66–68
assignments. *See* assessment
  activities
attendance policies, 3–4, 46–47, 87,
  115n10
authority and the syllabus, 41–42

Backward Design, 116n16
Bali, Maha, 82, 83
banking model of education, 41
Barton, Michelle A., 35, 37
Behling, Kirsten T., 67
believing (in) students, practice of,
  11–12
Birt, Jamie, 108n2
Boggs, Grace Lee, 26
boundaries: catch-up days and, 30;
  community and, 32–35; commuting
  and, 28–29; eating, rest, and,
  29–30; email and, 27; "guarding
  your yes," 30–31; importance of,
  2; pedagogical development and,
  26–27; social media and, 33–34;
  time off and, 28
"Bread and Roses" (Oppenheim),
  111n24
Bringing History Home program,
  5–6
Brooks, René, 31
brown, adrienne maree, 26
building a welcome. *See* welcome,
  building a
Burkeman, Oliver, 19

care: collective, 35–38; concept
of, 16–17; gender and, 113n40;
necessity of, 101, 103; structures of,
24. *See also* self-care
catch-up days and boundaries, 30
Cavanaugh, Sarah Rose, 36
Cervantez, Tianna, 6
cheating, 115n9
Chu, Gary, 76
classrooms: building a welcome in,
82–90; fear and self-knowledge
in, 100; participatory learning
and, 91–94; resolving tension and
conflict in, 81–82, 94–100. *See also*
welcome, building a
Cohan, Deborah, 62
community building, 32–38, 85,
91–92, 102–3, 112n31. *See also*
mutual aid
commuting and boundaries, 28–29
compassion, 2, 8, 11, 12, 62, 100
"Compassion Fund," 37
conflict resolution in the classroom,
81–82, 94–100
content warnings, 99–100, 127n39,
128n42
Costa, Karen, 37
course design. *See* assessment
activities; Universal Design for
Learning (UDL)
course policy language and the
syllabus, 45–47
Cozolino, Louis, 111n23
"Critical Reflexivity as a Tool for
Students" (Fernández), 21
curiosity and learning, 80, 88, 103,
111n23
currie, sarah madoka, 89–90

Designing for Care (Zamora and
Zamora), 83
Dialogue. *See* Intergroup Dialogue
Digital Pedagogy Lab (University of
Mary Washington), 8–9, 41, 43, 87
disability. *See* ableism
Domain of One's Own (University of
Mary Washington), 112n36

eating and boundaries, 29–30
educators: boundaries and,
25–36; positionality and, 21–22;
preparation of, 19–21; self-reflection
and, 24–25; social identities and,
21–23. *See also* self-care
email and boundaries, 27
Emergent Strategy (brown), 26
emotion: classrooms and, 92, 95–97;
presence of, 35–36, 101
equity, 7, 76, 92–93, 99, 102;
intentional equitable hospitality
(IEH), 82–83

Fasheh, Munir, 71
feedback, 68, 72–76, 120n18, 121n32.
See also assessment activities
Fernández, Jesica Siham, 21, 114n3
Fillpot, Elise, 5
Fiorenza, Elizabeth Schüssler,
106n11
Fisher, Roger, 97
forgiveness, 18, 39, 98
Freire, Paulo, 41
Friend, Chris, 41, 43, 55

Gabert-Quillen, Crystal A., 114n4
Gagné, Ann, 55
Gannon, Kevin, 44
Godbee, Beth, 31
grading: arbitrariness of, 71–73;
feedback and, 74–76; transparent
assignment design and, 79;
ungrading and, 73–74. *See also*
assessment activities
Gray, Brenna Clarke, 91
"guarding your yes" and boundaries,
30–31

Hanley, Devin, 6
harm prevention and repair work,
98–99
Harrington, Christine M., 114n4
"hidden curriculum" and assessment,
62–63
Hoang, Kylie, 55–56
Hogan, Kelly A., 80, 85

Hollis, James, 31–32
honor codes, 45–46
hooks, bell, 2
"How to Host a Restorative Dinner
    Party for Your Chosen Queer Fam"
    (Win), 33

icebreaker activities (warm-ups),
    88–89
Immordino-Yang, Mary Helen, 36
inadequacy, sense of, 21, 24–25
intentional equitable hospitality
    (IEH), 82–83. See also equity
Intergroup Dialogue, 6–7, 92, 97,
    106n6, 110n17

Jack, Jordynn, 62, 63
Jones, Christopher, 120n21
justice, 9–11, 39, 48–50, 98

Kaba, Mariame, 37
Kahn, Bill, 35
Kalir, Remi, 56
Kennedy, Robert F., 102
kindness: accountability and,
    100, 103; applications of,
    13–14; as discipline, 2, 12, 104;
    misconceptions of, 1–2; self-care
    and, 18
King, Jina B., 17
knowledge, transmission of, 38–39,
    63–64, 118n7
Kodipady, Aditi, 124n12
kyriarchy, 9, 106n11

laziness, 84
learning and curiosity, 80, 88, 103,
    111n23
learning goals, 50–52
learning management systems (LMS)
    and welcoming classrooms, 83–85
lectures, 4–5, 20, 42–43, 93
Lorde, Audre, 17

MacDonald, Kris, 10
Maitlis, Sally, 35
Marama, Yamiko, 16, 17

Masland, Lindsay C., 73
meditation, 8
Mejia, Donna, 41–42
mental health, 4, 7–8, 99, 106n6,
    109n6. See also content warnings;
    trauma
Miceli, Heather, 76–77
mindfulness, 8
Monopoly (board game), 112n30
Morris, Sean Michael, 41, 43, 55
Mowreader, Ashley, 57
mutual aid, 37–39, 89, 100. See also
    community building

niceness, 1–2, 11, 12, 36, 100–101
Noddings, Nel, 16, 18
Nye, Naomi Shihab, 8

Ocasio-Cortez, Alexandria, 37
O'Donnell, Daniel Paul, 69
office supplies and mutual aid, 38
Ohio State University, 36
On Repentance and Repair
    (Ruttenberg), 98
Oppenheim, James, 111n24
O'Reilley, Mary Rose, 86
Osario, Maricruz, 6

Pacansky-Brock, Michelle, 44–45, 85
Paredes, ChanTareya, 6
participatory learning, 91–94
pedagogy: adjusting approach
    to, 5; application of kindness
    to, 13–14; assumptions about,
    81; authority and, 3, 4–5, 9;
    believing (in) students and, 11–12;
    Bringing History Home and, 5–6;
    development of, 26–27; Digital
    Pedagogy Lab and, 8–9, 41, 43;
    graduate students and, 12–13;
    instructor preparation and, 19–21;
    Intergroup Dialogue and, 6–7;
    mutual aid and, 38–39; reaching
    students and, 80; reevaluation of,
    9; student input and, 55; teacher
    training and, 3
Peterson, Anne Helen, 29–30

Pletcher, Courtney, 55–56
polling, 93
positionality, 18, 21–22, 100
Price, Devon, 84

racial prejudice, 1
Raley-Karlin, Gabrielle, 6, 7, 23, 88
reconciliation, 18, 39
repair work and harm prevention,
    98–99
representation, 48, 114n3
resources for students, 48–50, 63,
    83–84
rest and boundaries, 29–30
rigor, academic, 2, 37, 62–63
rocks in the jar (parable), 19
Ruttenberg, Rabbi Danya, 98

Samaran, Nora, 113n40
Sarrouf, John, 96
Sathy, Viji, 62, 63, 80, 85
Schalk, Sami, 17
scheduling. See boundaries; syllabus
    design
Schinske, Jeffrey, 72–73, 120n25
scholarship of teaching and learning
    (SOTL), 26
Seale, Yvonne, 53
self-care: Google search of, 108n2;
    importance of, 39; institutional
    support for, 36; kindness toward
    the oneself and, 108n3; LMS
    resources for student, 83–84; as
    political act, 17–18; purposes of,
    15–16; wellness and, 35. See also
    boundaries; community building
self-reflection, 24–25, 76. See also
    social identity reflection chart
sexual violence, 7, 17, 99–100
skills. See knowledge, transmission of
SOCC (Source, Observe,
    Contextualize, and Corroborate), 6
social identity, 21–23
social identity reflection chart, 23–24
Social Justice Dialogues (Knox
    College), 18
social media, 33–34

Sorensen-Unruh, Clarissa, 61, 70–71,
    76
Spade, Dean, 37
Stains, Robert R., Jr., 96
"Stop Framing Wellness Programs
    around Self-Care" (Barton et al.), 35
student evaluations and diversity,
    105n3
students: as antagonists, 1, 3, 5, 9–10,
    12; critiques from, 4–5; diversity
    of, 10–11; equal treatment of, 7;
    expression of knowledge by, 61,
    68–69, 94; grading and self-
    reflection by, 75–77; graduate, 3,
    12, 19–20, 95–96, 101; on group
    work, 90; introductions of, 87–88;
    learning names of, 87, 125n18;
    participation suggestions from,
    92; practice of believing (in), 11;
    resources for, 48–50, 63, 83–84;
    social identity reflection by, 23–24,
    95–96; syllabus design input from,
    42, 55–56
Sutcliffe, Katherine M., 35
syllabus design: accessibility and,
    52–55; aims for, 57–58; course
    policy language and, 45–47;
    example of, 53, 54; images and
    graphic organizers in, 116n17;
    learning goals and, 50–52;
    legalistic language and, 40–41;
    length and, 114n4; reevaluation
    and, 9, 42–45, 57; as relational
    document, 41–42; representation,
    justice, and resources in, 48–50;
    spreadsheet templates and, 57;
    student participation in, 42, 55–57;
    Universal Design for Learning
    and, 67; welcoming students and,
    44–45
Syphers, David, 62

Tanner, Kimberley, 72–73, 120n25
teaching. See pedagogy
Teaching to Transgress (hooks), 2
time management, 15, 18–19, 50, 57,
    83

time off and boundaries, 28
Tobin, Thomas J., 67
Transparency in Learning and
    Teaching (TILT), 77
transparent assignment design,
    77–79
trauma, 63, 98–100, 102, 106n6. *See
    also* mental health
trigger warnings. *See* content
    warnings
Twitter (X) communities and
    academia, 33–34

unessay projects, 69–71
ungrading: definitions of, 73–74;
    educator concerns about, 77;
    student self-reflection and, 75–77;
    transparent assignment design
    and, 77–79
Universal Design for Learning (UDL),
    66–68, 89, 99–100
University of Michigan, 6, 18, 23, 92,
    93
University of Notre Dame, 37

Venet, Alex Shevrin, 109n6
Volpe, Allie, 34
vulnerability, 6–7

Wake Forest University, 57
warm-up activities (icebreakers),
    88–89
Warner, John, 73
welcome, building a: greeting
    students and, 85–86; group
    work and, 89–90; intentional
    equitable hospitality and, 82–83;
    introductions and, 87–88; pre-
    course contact and, 85; resources
    for students and, 82–85; student
    identification and, 124n12; student
    information and, 86–87; student
    names and, 87, 125n18; warm-ups
    and, 88–89
wellness, 35, 63. *See also* self-care
"Why Community Matters So
    Much—and How to Find Yours"
    (Volpe), 34
Win, Em, 33
Winkelmes, Mary-Ann, 77–78
writing and transmission of
    knowledge, 63–64, 69, 90, 94

Zamora, Mali, 83
Zamora, Mia, 83
Zera, Deborah, 7–8
Zúñiga, Ximena, 106n6

Printed in the USA
CPSIA information can be obtained
at www.ICGtesting.com
CBHW062022091124
17182CB00001B/1